THE DVD BOOK OF
SCOTLAND

Written by David Clayton

THE DVD BOOK OF
SCOTLAND

This edition first published in the UK in 2008
By Green Umbrella Publishing

www.gupublishing.co.uk

© Green Umbrella Publishing 2008

Publishers Jules Gammond and Vanessa Gardner

Printed and bound in China

ISBN 978-1-906229-66-5

Contents

Aitken Roy (1979 – 91)

Player stats:

Caps 57
Goals 1

BORN IN IRVINE, AYR-shire in 1958, Roy Aitken is one of Scottish football's best-loved sons. A promis-ing young talent, he signed schoolboy forms with his boyhood idols Celtic in 1970 and excelled in sev-eral other sports, particu-larly athletics, where he was both a school junior and senior Champion.

It was with Celtic, how-ever, that his name eventu-ally came to national prominence and the imposing centre-half quic-kly became a huge favourite at Parkhead, earning the nickname 'The Bear' and gaining a reputation as one of the toughest defenders in the country.

With the heart of a lion, he proudly represented Scotland 57 times between 1979 and 1991, making his debut as substitute during a 1-1 draw with Peru in September '79.

He scored just one goal for his coun-try and also played for Newcastle United, Aberdeen and St Mirren during his playing career.

After guiding Aberdeen to Scottish Cup success in 1995, Aitken then moved into coaching and joined David O'Leary at Leeds United and later at Aston Villa. Highly respected throughout the game, he was one of Alex McLeish's assistants for the Scottish national side before joining up with 'Big Eck' at Birmingham City in 2007. Unflinching and uncom-promising as a player, Aitken was a hardened warrior who served Scotland with great distinction.

Anfield

SCOTLAND'S BID TO REACH THE World Cup finals in Argentina came down to a nerve-wracking all or nothing Group decider at Liverpool's Anfield stadium in 1977. The Tartan Army invaded Merseyside in their thousands and Stanley Park became an impromptu temporary campsite prior to the match and would later be nicknamed 'Skol Island' by locals! The scenario was fairly simple – Scotland had to win to guarantee a place in the finals – a draw would have put them on five points with Wales on three and still one game to play. Both sides had a plus one goal difference and the only other side in the three-team group, Czechoslovakia, were out of contention. Wales needed a bigger venue than Cardiff's Ninian Park or Wrexham's Racecourse Ground with the capacity at both not able to meet the demand for tickets. Switching the match to what was in effect a neutral venue backfired on the Welsh, due to the huge numbers of 'travelling fans', who made Anfield into a mini-Hampden. On an incredibly tense evening and still no goals with 79 minutes on the clock,

French referee Robert Wurtz adjudged Lou Macari's cross to have been handled by a Wales defender in the box. Replays later proved it was Joe Jordan's arm, but the Tartan Army wasn't complaining and Don Masson coolly scored from the penalty spot. The Welsh, still furious with the decision, lost their shape and focus and eight minutes later Anfield was again shaken to the foundations as Kenny Dalglish – playing on home soil – added a second to send Ally MacLeod's boys to Argentina.

LEFT Roy Aitken in action
BELOW Scotland's Victory at Anfield earned them qualification for the 1978 World Cup finals in Argentina

Argentina

OF ALL THE WORLD CUP TOURNAments Scotland have qualified for over the years, none perhaps is more memorable than Argentina '78. Widely regarded as one of the greatest World Cups ever, Scotland played their part to the full, though it was a bittersweet experience for the Tartan Army to say the least.

On paper, the group draw had been kind, and though the strongly-fancied Holland were in Scotland's qualifying pool, rank outsiders Iran and Peru were also included. Manager Ally MacLeod had arguably assembled Scottish football's golden generation of players, and with the likes of Archie Gemmill, Graeme Souness, Kenny Dalglish, Willie Johnstone, Gordon McQueen, Joe Jordan, Asa Hartford and Willie Donachie to call upon, the opening Group 4 game against Peru in Cordoba looked winnable – on paper.

The Peruvians, however, were anything but push-overs and despite Jordan scoring the opening goal, Peru, inspired by the brilliant Teofilo Cubillas, deservedly ran out 3-1 winners. It was a disastrous start and the fall-out was, as expected, dramatic and emotional – and it got worse when winger Willie Johnstone was sent home in disgrace after failing a urine test for using banned substances. Nothing less than a victory over minnows Iran four days later would do, with Holland being the final group game. Again played in Cordoba, it was another disastrous outcome with Scotland held to a 1-1 draw, despite McLeod's men again taking a first-half lead, courtesy of an Iranian player, Andranik Eskandarian. Enough was enough for the army of Scots who had followed their team to Argentina, and they made their protests long and loud, demanding their money back because of their team's inept performances. Ally MacLeod had watched the Iran game like a man doomed for the gallows and with what seemed an inevitable defeat to the Dutch still to come, it appeared his days in the job were countable on one hand.

Yet despite the misery and controversy surrounding the team, the Holland match turned out to be one of the greatest triumphs by any Scotland team ever, with the talented squad finally realising its potential in one of the most breathtaking World Cup

matches ever. Needing to beat the Dutch by three goals, Scotland's mission impossible began to take on colossal proportions when Robert Rensenbrink scored from the penalty spot –four goals were now required against a team yet to concede at the tournament! Yet, a minute before the break, Dalglish equalised to give a glimmer of hope – and two minutes after the break, Archie Gemmill scored from the spot to make it 2-1 – the dream was still alive. The best, however, was yet to come. On 68 minutes Gemmill scored the goal of his life and one of the best ever at a World Cup, racing down the right, nutmegging a defender and then firing home over the advancing keeper to make it 3-1 with 22 minutes to play. It was fairytale stuff and one more goal would complete perhaps the greatest recovery ever seen – but just three minutes later, Johnny Rep scored a wonderful 30-yarder to make it 3-2 and there were no more goals.

Scotland were eliminated on goal difference and while pride may have been restored by such an exhilarating display, most Scottish fans were left wondering about what might have been.

Baxter (1960 – 67)

ONE OF SCOTTISH FOOTBALL'S favourite sons, James Curran Baxter was born on September 29, 1939 in Hill of Beath, Fife. Nicknamed 'Slim Jim', Baxter was a mercurial winger, a superb talent who was the darling of the Tartan Army for the best part of a decade. He began his career with Raith Rovers before moving to his boyhood idols Rangers in 1960 for what was then a Scottish transfer record of £17,500. Baxter spent five memorable years at Ibrox, breaking into the national team in November 1960 and winning his first cap against Northern Ireland. Baxter became a regular for his country for the next seven years, but it was two unforgettable displays against England that most endeared Baxter to Scotland supporters. In April 1963, he scored both goals in a 2-1 win at Wembley while in 1967 he gave a sensational display dur-

Player stats:

Caps	34
Goals	3

LEFT Jim Baxter

FAR LEFT Archie Gemmill scores against the Netherlands during the 1978 World Cup

ing a 3-2 win against the Auld Enemy – again at Wembley, making it all the sweeter. It was England's first defeat since winning the World Cup and Baxter famously did a spot of 'keepy-uppy' in the penalty area to infuriate the English players and fans while further enhancing his reputation North of the Border! Baxter played for Sunderland and Nottingham Forest before returning to Rangers for one last hurrah, though he was by this time a pale shadow of the talent that had once terrorised the best defences in the world. His off-field lifestyle was as colourful as his playing career, with women, booze and gambling eventually taking their toll and he retired aged only 30 in 1970. Several years ago, in response to a question about how he would handle the wages top players are paid today and whether it would have changed the way he'd lived his life, Baxter said: "Definitely. I'd have spent £50,000 a week at the bookies instead of £100."

He was a one-off – an entertainer and a genius that Scottish football will never forget. Baxter sadly died in April 2001 after a long battle against cancer.

Beattie, Andy
(Manager 1954 & 1959-60)

ANDY BEATTIE MAY NOT BE A NAME that is instantly recognised by Scotland fans, but his importance is worthy of note, nonetheless. In 1954, Beattie was installed as Scotland's first manager, despite the national team having existed since 1872! Before that, the team was selected by a board and, apparently, the system worked well enough for there to be no figurehead as such until the '54 World Cup in Switzerland. Beattie had experience in management with Barrow, Stockport County and Huddersfield, but nothing could have prepared him for his first brief spell in international football. The tournament was an unmitigated disaster from start to finish with Scotland's preparation nothing short of shambolic. The 1954 World Cup is covered in greater detail elsewhere in this book, but Beattie had to put up with a 13-man squad (the limit was 22 but the SFA decided 13 would be sufficient) and no training kit. Despite everything, Beattie's side only narrowly lost 1-0 to Austria, but the manager had had enough and before he had more damage inflicted on his reputation, he resigned, just prior to the second game against Uruguay – Scotland went on to lose 7-0. He returned for another 18-month spell in charge in 1959, but resigned the following year due to club commitments with Nottingham Forest.

Manager stats:	
P	17
W	5
D	4
L	11
F	25
A	35

Boyd, Tommy (1990 – 2001)

Player stats:

Caps   72
Goals   1

RIGHT Tommy Boyd in action during the World Cup qualifying match against Morocco

FAR RIGHT Graeme Souness and David Narey challenging Socrates of Brazil, 1982

AGED 24, FORMER CELTIC SKIPPER Tommy Boyd made his debut for Scotland as a substitute during a 2-1 victory over Romania. It would be the first of 72 caps Boyd earned for his country over an 11-year period, in which time he became a Scottish legend. He would captain his country on five occasions, none more so proudly than during a magnificent 1-0 win in Germany in 1997, though the next match was arguably his most disappointing experience as skipper – a 2-0 home defeat to Australia!

The Glasgow-born defender, equally at home at left-back or central defence, initially made his name with unfashion-able Motherwell and was part of a team that lifted the Scottish Cup for only the second time in the club's history. His solid, consistent displays earned him a big-money move south, with Chelsea paying £800,000 for his services in 1991. After an injury-hampered year in London, he returned North of the Border and joined Celtic for a fee of £750,000, embarking on a successful 11-year career with the Bhoys. Scotland's fifth most-capped player, Boyd was awarded the MBE in 2002 for his out-standing services to football.

Brazil

BRAZIL HAVE NEVER LOST TO Scotland in nine meetings, but despite both countries' proud international heritage, it wasn't until June 1966 that they first played each other. The game ended 1-1 at Hampden Park in front of almost 75,000 fans, Steve Chalmers scoring the hosts' goal. Six years later the sides met in Rio during the Brazilian Independence Cup with only skipper Billy Bremner a survivor from the first encounter. On this occasion, Brazil won 1-0 in front of 130,000 fanatical fans at the Estadio Maracana. Bremner was skipper for the next two clashes – a 1-0 home defeat in 1973 and an impressive 0-0 draw at the 1974 World Cup. Another 2-0 friendly defeat in Rio followed in 1977, followed by the heaviest loss ever against the Samba kings, a 4-1 hammering in Seville during the 1982 World Cup. Brazil maintained their unbeaten record at Hampden with a 2-0 Rous Cup win in 1987, and the teams were again pitted against each other in the 1990 and 1998 World Cup finals in Italy and France respectively. Brazil's winning margin was a solitary goal on each occasion.

Player stats:	
P	9
W	0
D	2
L	7
F	3
A	14

Bremner, Billy (1965 – 74)

RIGHT Billy Bremner and Francis Munro wait for a cross

DETERMINATION, ABILITY AND AGG-ression – three key components of Billy Bremner's make-up, and he is one of the few men in football to have genuinely earned the tag of 'legend'. One of Scotland's greatest players, Bremner was the heart and soul of the national team for almost a decade and wore the captain's armband in 39 of his 54 appearances. He may have been small in stature, but he had the heart of a warrior and his flame-red hair was a reflection of the fire that burned within – Bremner would shed blood for his country and wasn't capable of giving any less than one hundred per cent each time he pulled on the navy blue jersey.

Born in Stirling on December 9, 1942, Bremner, aged 16, joined Leeds United from school and within two years was a first-team player. It's no coincidence that Leeds enjoyed their glory years during Bremner's time at Elland Road, winning six major trophies in the space of six unforgettable years. He didn't win his first cap until he was 23 years old and after three years of battling midfield displays for Scotland, he was handed the captaincy. It's doubtful there was a prouder day in his career than when he led his country out for the first time against Denmark at the Idraetspark Stadium, Copenhagen. Scotland won 1-0 and kicked off Bremner's reign in suitable style – he would skipper the team for another six years and was an inspirational leader both on and off the pitch.

Bremner relished his tussles with 'the Auld Enemy' and would often go hell for leather against his Leeds United English team-mates, though he'd be the first to shake their hands at the end of 90 minutes. Bremner's influence on Scotland was perhaps never greater than when he helped steer his troops through the World Cup qualifiers to the 1974 finals in Germany. There, Scotland beat Zaire and then drew with both Brazil and Yugoslavia, only to go out of the tournament on goal difference.

Bremner retired from international football after the World Cup, though fittingly, his last game at Hampden Park was a 2-0 win over

ABOVE Billy Bremner and Colin Bell in a match against England, Wembley 1973

England. Curiously, Bremner never played club football in Scotland, but had spells with Doncaster and Hull as well as managing Leeds and Doncaster.

Booked just once in 54 games for Scotland, Bremner died in December 1992, two days shy of his 55th birthday. The Bremner legend, however, lives on.

Brown, Craig (1993 – 2001)

Manager stats:	
P	71
W	32
D	18
L	21
F	86
A	63 + 23

AFTER AN AVERAGE PLAYING CAREER, Craig Brown found his vocation in coaching and later, management. He began his career as a teenager with Rangers, but failed to break into the first team at Ibrox and moved on to Dundee where he remained for nearly five years. From there he went to Falkirk, but was plagued by knee injuries and finally retired as player in 1967, aged 27. It would be another seven years before he earned his first role of any note, becoming assistant boss at Motherwell in 1974. Three years later he became manager of Clyde on a part-time basis and remained with the club for a decade, juggling his 'day job' as a primary school head teacher and later a lecturer in primary education. In 1986 he returned to football on a full-time basis by being appointed as Andy Roxburgh's assistant for the Scottish national team as well as taking on various roles for Scotland's youth sides with great success. The SFA were impressed with Brown's achievements – so much so that when Roxburgh resigned in 1993, Brown took over as Scotland manager, initially on a caretaker basis, before earning the job permanently.

The quiet, unassuming and likeable Brown went on to steer Scotland successfully to Euro '96 and the World Cup finals at France '98, but his impressive run was ended when England triumphed over two legs in a Euro 2000 play-off – dubbed 'The Battle of Britain' in the media – despite a 1-0 victory for Brown's team at Wembley. A poor qualifying campaign for the 2002 World Cup spelled the end of Brown's reign as Scotland boss, though he clearly played a major part in raising the profile of Scottish international football once more.

Burley, George

(1979 – 82 & Manager Present)

RIGHT George Burley the current manager

FAR RIGHT George Burley in his playing days

IT'S NO REAL SURPRISE THAT George Burley eventually became Scotland boss. The former, Ipswich Town, Motherwell and Sunderland full-back has enjoyed a fair degree of success since moving into management and the sterling job he did during his brief, turbulent time with Hearts, opened a few eyes North of the Border to his ability to deal with even the most complicated of situations. During his playing days, Burley rose to prominence as part of an excellent Ipswich Town side and the highly-respected defender stayed for 12 years in Suffolk, clocking up more than 400 appearances. He later played for Sunderland, Gillingham, Motherwell (twice), Ayr, Falkirk and Colchester, moving into management with the latter in 1994. It seemed inevitable he would one day manage Ipswich and, after just six months with Colchester, he returned to the club he'd served so well as player. He spent a further eight years at Portman Road before taking over at Derby County, then managed Hearts, leaving the Tynecastle outfit top of the SPL with nine wins from their opening 12 games when he left, before taking over at Southampton. Burley won all 11 of his Scotland caps as an Ipswich Town player and made his debut against Wales in 1978 – the only mystery was why such a talented defender didn't win more.

Burns, Kenny (1974 – 81)

RIGHT Kenny Burns in action

GLASGOW-BORN KENNY BURNS was from the old school of Scottish footballers. Tough, fearless and uncompromising in the tackle, Burns perhaps earned fewer caps than he should have, mainly due to a mid-career positional change. He actually began his career at Rangers as a striker before being freed and joining Birmingham City where he earned a reputation as a hard-working forward. He won his first international cap while at St Andrew's, appearing as a forward during a 2-1 defeat to West Germany, though his next appearance was a happier occasion, as he scored what would be his only Scotland goal during a 3-0 win over East Germany. Brian Clough took him to Nottingham Forest in 1977 for £150,000 and con-verted the striker into a top-class cen-tre-half. In fact, Burns was the rock of Clough's all-conquering side of the 1970s and he captained the East Midlands outfit to, among other things, successive League titles and European Cup successes. Burns won recognition as a defender for his country, too and earned his 20th and final cap during the 1981 Home Internationals against Wales.

Captains

THERE HAVE BEEN 56 PLAYERS WHO have captained Scotland over the years, none more than George Young who led his country on 48 occasions between 1948 and 1957. Current captain Barry Ferguson, with 26 caps going into 2008, seems the most likely to threaten Young's record. Billy Bremner wore the armband on 38 occasions between 1968 and 1975 and Gary McCallister enjoyed

ABOVE Archie Gemmill

Player	Years	Captain
George Young	1948-57	48
Billy Bremner	1968-75	38
Gary McCallister	1993-99	32
Graeme Souness	1982-86	27
Roy Aitken	1976-81	27
Archie Gemmill	1960-90	23
Colin Hendry	1996-2001	23
Paul Lambert	1999-2003	17
Eric Cadlow	1960-63	15
John Grieg	1965-75	15

a six-year spell as skipper between 1993 and 1999. Roy Aitken and Graeme Souness both captained Scotland 27 times, while Archie Gemmill and Colin Hendry (both 23) are the only other players to lead the team more than 20 times. There are 14 players who skippered the side just once, Ally McCoist and Craig Levein among them. Left are the Top 10 armband-wearers.

supporters are Rod Stewart, Billy Connolly and Sean Connery. Stewart, though born in London, is of Scottish stock (his mum and dad were both born in Scotland) and he attends matches at Hampden or around the world whenever he gets the opportunity and can

Celebrities

ABOVE Sean Connery
RIGHT Billy Connolly

WHEN IT COMES TO CELEBRITY Scotland fans, obviously, the numbers are legion. Every Scottish rock star, actor, comedian or writer has a vested interest in the national team's progress, but perhaps the most famous Scotland

regularly be spotted heartily joining in terrace chants and songs. In 1978, he recorded the official Scotland World Cup song 'Ole, Ola' and his classic 'Sailing' is often belted out by the Tartan Army – quite a tribute considering his origins South of the Border! If Sean Connery watches Scotland from the stands, chances are you will see a picture of the former James Bond star in any one of a dozen tabloids. Billy Connolly, a resident of California for some years now, also flies the flag home and abroad whenever the opportunity arises. All three men are fiercely patriotic and also the nation's most famous football fans.

ABOVE Rod Stewart

Collins, John (1988 – 99)

Player stats:

Caps   58
Goals 12

WHEN TALK TURNS TO CULTURED Scottish midfielders, chances are John Collins will be at the forefront of most people's minds. Collins was one of Scotland's most gifted purveyors of the Beautiful Game and, for more than a decade, he added style and panache to the national team's engine room. Born in the rugby-mad area of Galashiels in January 1968, Collins fell in love with football from an early age. It was not long before SPL scouts were flocking to Hutcheson Vale to watch an outstanding talent ply his trade and, aged 16, Hibernian leapt to the front of the queue and signed the teenage protégé. He remained at Easter Road for six years, earning his first Scotland cap against Saudi Arabia in 1988.

Two years later he moved to Celtic where he enjoyed another six-year stint, by now a regular for both club and country. With an average better than a goal every six games for Scotland, he also played club football for Monaco and Everton, though injuries began to reduce the number of appearances he made domestically and internationally. His last game for Scotland, fittingly, was a 1-0 win against England at Wembley – his 58th cap, and after a spell with Fulham he retired in 2003 and until recently managed his first club, Hibs. Future national team boss? Watch this space.

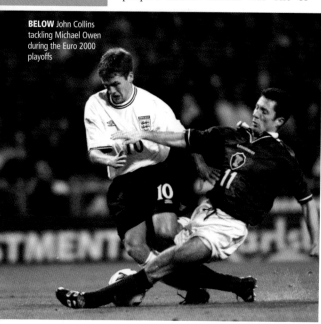

BELOW John Collins tackling Michael Owen during the Euro 2000 playoffs

Dailly, Christian
(1997 – Present)

LIKE A FINE WINE, CENTRAL DEF-ender/defensive midfielder Christian Dailly's international career has improved with the passage of time. At the time of writing, Dailly had just passed Willie Miller in the all-time appearances list for his country by earning his 66th cap against Ukraine – just 10 days shy of his 34th birthday. His international career began a decade earlier during a 1-0 home defeat to Wales and Dailly has since led Scotland a dozen times, the first occasion was memorable for the wrong reasons – a disastrous 4-1 defeat to South Korea! A succession of managers have called upon the dependable Dailly over the years and his ability to fill a variety of positions with equal aplomb has made

Player stats:

Caps: 66
Goals: 6

LEFT Christian Dailly in 1999

him an invaluable squad member to have around. His club career began with his hometown club Dundee and he represented Scotland at Under-21 level aged 16. He went on to win a record 34 caps for the youngsters – a world record – and later played for Derby County, Blackburn Rovers, West Ham and Southampton. Refreshingly, Dailly has never had an agent, preferring to negotiate his own deals without interference and though he is approaching the final years of his playing career, many believe he will one day move into management and enjoy equal success in years to come.

Dalglish, Kenny (1971 – 86)

IT WOULD BE HARD TO ARGUE that Kenny Dalglish isn't the greatest Scotland player ever and there would be few who would dare to even suggest as much – quite simply, he was one of football's true greats. Some believe, probably with justification that he never quite reached the same heights for his country as he did at club level, but even a slightly-underperforming Dalglish stood out a mile whenever he played. Born in the East End of Glasgow but raised in the docklands area of the city, Dalglish grew up supporting Rangers, so it was ironic that he should one day become a legend at arch-rivals Celtic, though he wasn't the first to excel for a boyhood enemy and certainly not the last, either. Beginning his playing career as a keeper, his natural ability soon shone through and he gradually began moving up the field as he got older. He had trials with West Ham and, remarkably, for Liverpool, then managed by the great Bill Shankly, but he slipped through the net each time and instead returned home to sign for Celtic in 1967. It would take four years for him to break through into the first team and when given a chance in a friendly by manager Jock Stein, he scored six of the Hoops' seven goals! From then on, Dalglish was rarely out of the senior side and in his first full season at

Player stats:

Caps 102
Goals 30

BELOW Kenny Dalglish

passed, he wrote his name into Celtic folklore. In 1977 he moved to Liverpool for a British record of £440,000 as a replacement for Kop idol Kevin Keegan – few could envisage that Dalglish would emulate Keegan and become an Anfield legend, helping the Merseysiders to almost complete domination of English and European competitions for a decade. After a disappointing first World Cup in 1974, much was expected of Dalglish at the 1978 finals, but despite scoring in a remarkable 3-2 win over Holland, it was something of an anti-climax for Dalglish and the rest of the Scotland team.

He briefly captained the side in the late Seventies before handing the armband over to Archie Gemmill, and continued playing for his country well into the 1980s, equalling Denis Law's record of 30 goals with a strike in a 2-1 win over Spain in 1984. He led Scotland one final time as he won his one hundredth cap in a 3-0 win over Romania and won two more caps before hanging up his international boots for the last time and moving into an equally successful management career, most notably with Liverpool and Blackburn Rovers. A remarkable talent.

Parkhead, the 21-year-old forward won his first Scotland cap during a 1-0 win over Belgium.

Dalglish was a master craftsman, a genius on the ball with an almost unique ability to hold on to it and bring others into play. He had vision and superb technique and as the years

Docherty, Tommy

(1951 – 59 & Manager 1972 – 72)

CHARISMATIC, OCCASIONALLY CONtroversial, but never dull, Tommy Docherty served club and country with distinction, though the lure of manag-

ing Manchester United would mean he cut short his tenure as national team boss. Born in Glasgow, Docherty's first professional club was Celtic, but his ambition to play in England meant his stay at Parkhead was a brief one and he travelled south to play for Preston North End. He played in Scotland's first World Cup in Switzerland and later helped skipper his country to World Cup qualification in 1958, but was promptly dropped from the squad that travelled to Sweden! He moved to Arsenal in 1958 and was recalled for national duty shortly after. After ending his playing career at Chelsea, he became manager at Stamford Bridge from 1961 to 1967 – the first of 16 jobs in management spanning 27 years. 'The Doc', as he is known throughout football, once quipped that he'd had more clubs than golfer Jack Nicklaus. He became Scotland boss in 1971 and lost just three of his first 12 games in charge. However, when Manchester United approached him to take over at Old Trafford, Docherty couldn't resist a crack with the Reds and he quit his post to return to club football, leaving supporters North of the Border to wonder about what might have been…

Manager stats:

P	12
W	7
D	2
L	3
F	17
A	8

Player stats:

Caps	25
Goals	1

LEFT Tommy Docherty had a shortlived but very successful time as manager

BELOW Tommy Docherty won 25 Scottish caps during his career

Donachie, Willie (1972 – 78)

WILLIE DONACHIE PLAYED STEADILY at left-back for Scotland for six years,

playing twice at the 1978 World Cup finals and earning 35 caps along the way. Steady and reliable, Donachie was picked up by Manchester City as a junior and after breaking into the first team as a replacement for Glyn Pardoe, Donachie rarely missed a game for the Blues throughout the 1970s. He won his first cap against Peru in April 1972 and went on to make more than 350 appearances for City, scoring just two goals. In fact, goals were something of a rarity throughout his career and though he never found the net for his country, he did once score a goal at Hampden Park – in his own net! It's unfair that most people recall his 25-yard own goal against Wales in 1978 more than his consistency in Scotland's defence, but sometimes, that's just how it goes… Donachie left City in 1980 to play for Portland Timbers in America, before returning to play for Norwich City and Oldham Athletic. It was while with Oldham that he established himself as a coach of some repute and assisted Joe Royle for several years at both Boundary Park and Manchester City before managing Millwall until recently.

Player stats:

Caps: 35
Goals: 0

LEFT Willie Donachie was twice a member of the Scotland World Cup squad

England

Player stats:	
P	109
W	40
D	24
L	45
F	164
A	189

THERE IS NO FIXTURE OLDER IN world football than Scotland versus England. Perhaps the greatest rivals in international football, it is fitting that the 1872 clash between the two countries was the first recorded international match anywhere. That game, played at Hamilton Crescent in Glasgow, ended 0-0 – one of only three goalless draws in 109 clashes. Scotland's record win against 'the Auld Enemy' came in 1872, when the English were sent home having been thrashed 7-2 at Hampden Park and almost a decade later, the Scots recorded their record away win – 6-1 – played at the Kennington Oval, London.

The fixture always invokes a tremendous sense of national pride on both sides of the border, though it is the Scottish passion that has always shone brightest, particularly when the Tartan Army invariably takes over Wembley Stadium. The mini invasion during the 1977 clash when members of the Tartan Army dismantled much of England's home ground, including the pitch and goal posts, will live long in the memory! In international football, this game is undoubtedly the fiercest 'derby', though it is England who have edged the fixture

over the years with 45 wins to Scotland's 40. One of Scotland's sweetest victories was the 5-1 win at Wembley Stadium in 1928 where an Alex Jackson hat-trick and a brace from Alex James sent those North of the Border home in raptures. Record away defeats include a 9-3 loss in 1961 and a 7-2 reverse in 1955. England have twice won 5-0 in Scotland and the Euro 2000 play-off was also edged by the English who won the first leg 2-0 at Hampden Park while Scotland won 1-0 at Wembley in the return game. Always a fixture packed with passion and history, it is one of the most eagerly-awaited games anywhere in the world.

ABOVE Action from the match against England during the Euro 2000 play-offs

LEFT Players competing for the ball during an England v Scotland match at the Oval

European Championships

SCOTLAND'S EUROPEAN CHAMPionship history is a story of steady progression and continued improvement.

The first qualification game was against Wales in 1966, with an 86th minute goal from Denis Law earning a 1-1 draw, though it would be 26 years before Scotland actually appeared at the European Championship finals for the Sweden '92 tournament. Though knocked out in the group stages,

Scotland again qualified for Euro '96, held of course in England, but again the Tartan Army were left disappointed following elimination in the group stages. For the next two tournaments, there was further heartbreak for Scottish fans, with the agony of play-off defeats denying Scotland the chance to progress to the 2000 and 2004 final stages. In 1999, in a match dubbed 'The Battle of Britain', Scotland took on England over two legs. The damage was done at Hampden Park, where the English triumphed 2-0 and despite a heroic 1-0 win at Wembley, England held on to win a place at Euro 2000. In 2004,

Scotland were again faced with a two-legged play-off, this time against Holland, for the right to play at the 2004 finals. James McFadden's solitary strike gave Scotland hope and a 1-0 into the second leg, but the Dutch were unstoppable in Amsterdam and the scoring was complete with just 67 minutes – with the score 6-0 to Holland and Scottish dreams in tatters. There was further heartache in 2007, when, despite a magnificent campaign that included two wins over France, Scotland were robbed of qualification by a last-minute winner for Italy in the final game at Hampden.

ABOVE Barry Ferguson celebrates after scoring during qualifying

LEFT Tempers run high during the World Cup qualifier match against Sweden, 1997

Ferguson, Alex
(Manager 1986)

Manager stats:	
P	10
W	3
D	4
L	3
F	8
A	5 + 3

THE EVENTS LEADING UP TO ALEX Ferguson's brief reign as Scotland manager arguably convinced the then Aberdeen manager that perhaps the national team hot-seat brought with it intense pressure and expectation that he just wasn't ready for. The tragic death of Jock Stein during a World Cup qualifier with Wales in September 1985 meant that Scotland, who had secured the point they'd needed, progressed to Mexico '86 without a manager. The team needed a strong character to guide them through a particularly tough group stage and the hottest talent in the country at that time was undoubtedly Ferguson, who had broken the Celtic/Rangers domination of the SPL by guiding Aberdeen to three titles in eight years.

Stein's death had left a huge void in Scottish football and, arguably, Ferguson was on a hiding to nothing, risking his reputation as one of British football's brightest managerial prospects – yet he accepted the role when asked.

Pitted against West Germany, Uruguay and Denmark, the Govan-born Ferguson had little time to plan or work with his squad and Scotland controversially lost their opening game to Denmark 1-0. It was hard to swallow, especially as the referee had disallowed what had seemed a perfectly good goal by Roy Aitken. The next game against West Germany was a must-win match if Scotland were to

ABOVE Alex Furguson had a very brief reign as Scotland manager

have the chance of progressing further and when Gordon Strachan scored on 17 minutes, the Tartan Army dared to dream. Four minutes later and Rudi Völler had equalised and five minutes after the break Klaus Allofs made it 2-1 – enough to win the game for the Germans. With no hope of qualification, Scotland played out a 0-0 draw with Uruguay before flying home again. The Scottish FA tried to tempt Ferguson to take the job permanently, but he'd already decided to take on the job at Manchester United, where he remains to this day.

He is believed to have turned down the opportunity to manage his country several times since…

Ferguson, Barry

(2000 – Present)

Player stats:

Caps   42
Goals 2

RIGHT Barry Feguson in action during the World Cup qualifier against Belarus, 2005

FAR RIGHT Ferguson tackles Andriy Nesmachny of the Ukraine during the Euro 2008 Group B qualifying match

BARRY FERGUSON IS WELL ON HIS way to joining an elite band of Scotland players to have earned 50 caps or more during their international career and, but for injury, he'd have comfortably exceeded that number several years ago. The skillful Rangers midfielder has skippered his country on more than 25 occasions after making his debut against Lithuania in 1998 aged 20. Born February 2, 1978 in Hamilton, Ferguson would follow in the footsteps of his older brother Derek by playing for his boyhood idols Rangers, though Barry has eclipsed even his brother's achievements by becoming one of the most popular Rangers players of modern times. It is a measure of his popularity at Ibrox that after being stripped of the captaincy and then dropped by manager Paul Le Guen in January 2007, it was Le Guen who was quickly heading for the exit door a day later, with Ferguson reclaiming the armband shortly after. He skippered his country through the ultimately unsuccessful 2006 World Cup qualifying stages, hav-

ing first been appointed by Bertie Vogts and Walter Smith and his successor Alex McLeish – both of whom have had Ferguson as their club captain at Rangers – and both of whom continued to employ Ferguson as the national team captain. His only two goals to date have come against the Republic of Ireland and the Faroe Islands and Ferguson is expected to keep the armband under new boss George Burley.

France

Match stats:	
P	15
W	8
D	0
L	7
F	15
A	20

SCOTLAND HAVE A PROUD RECORD against the French, but it was the two victories in the European Championship qualifiers in 2006 and 2007 that will live long in the memory. The first game played between the two countries was back in 1930, when Scotland triumphed in Paris 2-0. Two years later and Scotland won in Paris again, this time by a score of 3-1. By 1951, France had been beaten in five of the six meetings against Scotland, though redressing the balance somewhat, the French dominated the fixture between 1958 and 2002, winning six out of seven meetings, including their only win to date at Hampden Park in March 2000. The biggest winning margin in this fixture saw France romp

home 5-0 in Paris in 2002, but it is Gary Caldwell's and James McFadden's solitary strikes in the two single-goal victories in the Euro 2008 qualifiers that gave the Tartan Army the most pleasure, particularly when Scotland's chances had been written off by many before a ball had even been kicked.

Gallacher, Kevin (1998 – 2008)

RIGHT Kevin Gallacher in action against Holland,1996

GRANDSON OF FORMER CELTIC legend Patsy Gallacher, Kevin Gallacher was universally popular at both international and club level and he enjoyed a fruitful playing career that spanned almost 20 years.

Under the stewardship of Jim McLean, the Clydebank-born forward established himself as one of Scottish football's hottest properties while at Dundee United.

A firm fans' favourite, he stayed at Tannadice for seven years, winning his first Scotland cap against Colombia in 1987 thereafter becoming a permanent fixture for his country. In 1990 he moved to Coventry City where he again proved a hit on the terraces.

His effervescent, all-action style was both exciting and full of passion and he was an asset to any side's forward line, and in 1993 he moved to Blackburn Rovers for £1.5m. Gallacher never let his country down and successfully transferred his domestic form to international football and largely thanks to his prolific scoring (six goals in eight matches) during the 1998 World Cup qualifiers that enabled Scotland to play at France '98. Gallacher led his country on one occasion, during a 2-0 win over San Marino in 2000, and made his last appearance for the national side six months later against the same team. Gallacher is now a TV and radio pundit.

Gemmill, Archie

(1971 – 81)

Player stats:

Caps 43
Goals 8

ARCHIE GEMMILL'S ILLUSTRIOUS career could never be accused of being dull and he will be forever remembered by Scottish fans for scoring THAT goal against the Dutch in the 1978 World Cup. Gemmill made his international debut in February 1971 against Belgium, having carved out a successful club career with St Mirren and Preston between 1964 and 1970. It was when he joined Derby County, however, that Gemmill's star really began to rise and under the stewardship of Brian Clough, who threatened to sleep in a car outside his house if he didn't sign for the Rams, Gemmill broke into Scotland's side and would quickly become an influential figure for his country over the next decade, taking on the captaincy in 1976 and leading Scotland to five wins in his first games as skipper. He wore the armband 21 times in total and was on the losing on only six occasions – an excellent record and one of the best in Scotland's history.

An industrious and wholehearted midfield schemer, it was at Argentina '78 that Gemmill (who also has the distinction of being Scotland's first-ever substitute) came to the attention of world football. Having put his country 2-1 from the spot against Holland in the final group game, he collected the ball outside the Dutch box on 68 minutes, played a one-two with Kenny Dalglish, nutmegged a defender before chipping the ball over the keeper to make it 3-1. Following disastrous displays against Peru and Iran, Scotland's chances had been all but written off, but now, needing a three-goal winning margin and leading 3-1, the nation began to dream of a miracle. It was not just one of the tournament's great goals, it was one of the best ever, but sadly it proved in vain and the Dutch progressed despite having lost the game 3-2.

The goal, however, will never be forgotten and remains one of the high points of Scotland's history. Gemmill, meanwhile, moved from Derby to Nottingham Forest and he led his country for the final time a day after his 34th birthday in March 1981. He continued playing club football for another three years, enjoying spells with Birmingham City, Jacksonville, Wigan Athletic and Derby County before moving into

coaching alongside his long-time mentor Brian Clough at Nottingham Forest. Gemmill is now the head coach of the Scotland Under-20 side and his son Scot represented the senior side on 26 occasions between 1995 and 2002.

Gilzean, Alan

(1963 – 71)

RIGHT Alan Gilzean appeared twenty two times for the Scotland team

ON A GOALS-PER-GAME RATIO FOR Scotland, Alan Gilzean's strike record is up among the very best. Better than one every two games, Coupar Angus-born Gilzean made his debut in a 6-1 win over Norway in 1963, though ironically was not among the scorers that day. Then a Dundee player, he scored his first Scotland goal in a 1-0 win over the English at Hampden Park in 1964 before taking part in a fundraising game for a Scotland select side against Tottenham Hotspur following the death of fellow Scot John White. Gilzean scored two goals at White Hart Lane during that game – and promptly found himself a new club South of the Border as Spurs snapped up the prolific forward for £72,500. Gilzean soon forged an excellent strike partnership with Jimmy Greaves and continued to represent his country with great effect, scoring twice on four different occasions, most memorably away to West Germany in 1964. Gilzean's final appearance for his country was in April 1971 against Portugal and he retired from club football three years later having appeared 343 times for Spurs and scored 93 goals.

Gough, Richard

(1983 – 93)

ABOVE Richard Gough tackles Gary Lineker during a Rous Cup match at Wembley, 1988

BUT FOR VOICING HIS OPINION ON national team coaches, Andy Roxburgh and Craig Brown, Richard Gough would surely be several places higher on the list of Scotland's most capped players. After winning 61 caps still aged only 31, Gough's criticism of the men who selected him meant he had little other choice but to retire from international football, though it's hard to imagine Gough arrived at that decision easily, having been the rock of the national team for almost exactly a decade.

His background was quite diverse, having been born in Stockholm to Scottish parentage and then raised in South Africa. His father, Charlie, had played for Charlton Athletic and during his teens, Richard won a provisional contract at The Valley. However, his heart was set on a career in his mother country and despite having an unsuccessful trial with Rangers, in 1980, the 18-year-old defender signed for Dundee United and enjoyed six years with the Tannadice club, breaking into the national side in 1983, before being snapped up by Tottenham Hotspur in 1986 for £750,000. Gough found it difficult to settle in the south and returned to Scotland after less than a year at White Hart Lane – ironically signing for Rangers for a record £1m – and would go on to become a club legend after spending 10 years at Ibrox and captaining the side seven of the nine successive SPL titles won during his time there. In 1991 he was handed the captain's armband for the clash with Russia and he would lead his country on another eight occasions and play at two World Cup finals and one European Championship. He became the member of a select club when he was sent off as captain during a 3-1 defeat to Switzerland in 1991. His last cap was against Portugal in April 1993 though he continued playing club football for various teams until 2001, moving briefly into management with Livingstone in 2004.

ABOVE Richard Gough tackles Gary Lineker during a Rous Cup match at Wembley, 1988

Player stats:

Caps	61
Goals	6

Gray, Andy

(1975 – 83)

DESPITE A MORE THAN USEFUL record at club level, Andy Gray's international career never really took off. He won an average of two caps a year following his 1975 debut against Romania and managed seven goals during a decade of football for his country. Ask any Dundee, Aston Villa, Wolves or Everton fan why Gray didn't win double the amount of caps he actually did and chances are they will be lost for an answer. Gray, a typical old-fashioned centre-forward, hard as nails and lethal in the air did have the

likes of Joe Jordan and Kenny Dalglish blocking his path, it's true, but for some reason he could never win a regular starting place in the squad regardless of his scoring feats for a succession of club sides.

He was never selected to play in either the 1974, 1978, 1982 or 1986 World Cup finals and it's hard to imagine that he doesn't look back with some wonderment as to why that was. Gray moved into a successful career in the media following his retirement and is now among the best-paid and respected football commentators on British TV with his phrases 'Right on cue' and 'Take a bow son' now part of the British football language.

Gray, Eddie

(1969 – 76)

Player stats:

Caps 12
Goals 3

RIGHT Eddie Gray in his footballing days with Leeds

FAR RIGHT Frank Gray won thirty two Caps for Scotland

ONE OF THE GREATEST WINGERS of his era, Eddie Gray must look back at his haul of international caps and wonder where it all went wrong.

A succession of badly-timed injuries undoubtedly robbed him of more than the dozen he actually earned, but even so, for a player who played in the great Leeds United team of the early Seventies, 12 caps is a meagre return for one of Scotland's most successful exports. Born in Glasgow and a Scottish schoolboy international, Gray would go on to become the archetypal one-club man, playing for Leeds from 1965 to 1983, making almost 600 appearances for the Elland Road side. He made his debut for Scotland aged 21, though it was memorable for all the wrong reasons – a 4-1 defeat to England. A week later, however, he won his second cap and was among the scorers in an 8-0 win over Cyprus. After earning his eighth cap in two years against Holland in 1971, he would have to wait another five years before he played for his country again. He was selected for the 1974 World Cup, but had to withdraw through injury – the bane of his wonderful career. He won his last cap in November 1976 and retired from playing in 1984 after a spell as Leeds' player/manager.

Gray, Frank

(1976 – 83)

FRANK GRAY SERVED CLUB AND country with great distinction during the Seventies and Eighties, winning 32 caps for Scotland. The younger brother of Scottish winger Eddie Gray, Frank was signed on by Leeds United and made his debut aged 18 for the Elland Road side. He began life as a midfielder but would eventually establish himself as a left-back and in 1976 was selected for his country for the first time. He made his debut against Switzerland in a 1-0 victory, but it would be a further three years before he played for Scotland again. He moved from Leeds to Nottingham Forest and became the first player to play in two European Cup finals for different English clubs when Forest beat Hamburg in 1981, by which time he had become a regular in the national team, playing 31 times in the space of four years, including all three of Scotland's World Cup matches at Spain '82 – as a Leeds United player having rejoined the Lilywhites in 1981. He made his final Scotland appearance during a 3-0 win against Canada in

1983, still aged only 29, and racked up almost 300 more club appearances in the nine years that followed, suggesting he was perhaps discarded a little early from the international scene. Frank's son, Andy, has so far won one Scotland cap.

Player stats:	
Caps	32
Goals	1

Hall Of Fame

RIGHT Hampden Park

IN FEBRUARY 1988, THE SFA LAUNched an International Roll of Honour, initially comprising the first 11 Scottish players to have made 50 international appearances. Each member receives a gold medal, an invitation for life to all Scotland's home matches, and has his portrait hung at the Scottish Football Museum. Only 25 players have made the list so far.

Player	From	To	Goals	Caps	Player	From	To	Goals	Caps
Dalglish, Kenny	1971	1986	30	102	McAllister, Gary	1990	1999	5	57
Leighton, Jim	1982	1998	0	91	Law, Dennis	1958	1974	30	55
McLeish, Alex	1980	1993	0	77	Malpas, Maurice	1984	1992	0	55
McStay, Paul	1983	1997	9	76	Bremner, Billy	1965	1975	3	54
Boyd, Tom	1990	2001	1	72	Souness, Graeme	1974	1986	4	54
Dailly, Christian	1997	2007	6	66	Gallacher, Kevin	1988	2001	9	53
Miller, Willie	1975	1989	1	65	Rough, Alan	1976	1986	0	53
McGrain, Danny	1973	1982	0	62	Young, George	1946	1957	0	53
Gough, Richard	1983	1993	6	61	Jordan, Joe	1973	1982	11	52
McCoist, Ally	1986	1998	19	61	Hendry, Colin	1993	2001	3	51
Weir, David	1997	2007	1	61	Hartford, Asa	1972	1982	4	50
Collins, John	1988	1999	12	58	Strachan, Gordon	1980	1992	5	50
Aitken, Roy	1979	1991	1	57					

Hampden Park

HOME TO SCOTTISH FOOTBALL FOR more than a century, Hampden Park is one of the most famous football arena's in world football and a place where many a team has shrivelled under the blast of the Hampden Roar, which can be heard up to seven miles away, so it is said. Until 1950, Hampden was the biggest stadium in the world and once boasted an incredible capacity of 183,724 (1937), though due to safety regulations the capacity today is less than a third of that figure – 52,103. Home to Scottish league side Queen of the South, the current Hampden Park, built in 1903, is the third stadium to bear the name, while the previous two Hampdens became homes to the Hampden Bowling Club (first Hampden) and Third Lanark FC (second Hampden). Scotland played their first game at the new Hampden on April 7, 1906 when 102,741 fans witnessed a 2-1 win over England, James Howie scoring both goals for the hosts who wore a strip of primrose and pink hoops, no less.

The stadium holds a number of notable 'firsts' in world football includ-

LEFT Hampden Park taken during the UEFA match between Scotland and Germany, 2003

ing turnstiles, a press box, a public address system and an on-site car park – all of which originally appeared at the home of Scottish football. It also boasts a European attendance record for the 1937 clash against England when no less than 149,415 people crammed in. The stadium was largely rebuilt and vastly improved during the 1990s and today it is one of only two five-star UEFA-graded stadiums in Scotland – the other being Ibrox – and though there have been occasions when a completely new ground has been mooted, the people of Scotland have always vociferously protested against a move from what many people believe to be the spiritual home of football. There is, quite simply, no destination as daunting as a packed and partisan Hampden Park in world football – and that's not something the Tartan Army is about to give up easily.

Hansen, Alan
(1979 – 87)

IT IS REMARKABLE THAT ONE OF the most important members of the all-conquering Liverpool team of the Seventies and Eighties represented his country on so few occasions. In a career spanning 17 successful years, Alloa-born Alan Hansen played just 26 times for Scotland, largely due to the successful partnership of Aberdeen's Alex McLeish and Willie Miller both at domestic and international level. Both players were the chosen central defensive pairing for several years and despite the elegant, effective and intelligent performances Hansen made at club level, he was all but ignored by a succession of international managers.

He began his career at Partick Thistle, staying at Firhill for four years until Liverpool stole a march on a host of top sides watching his progress. The Merseysiders paid just £110,000 for his services – arguably one of the best transfer fees they ever paid – and Hansen was soon the mainstay of a superb Anfield side, winning title after title, trophy after trophy. Jock Stein gave

Player stats:

Caps	26
Goals	0

ABOVE The European Cup trophy is raised in triumph by three of the scotsmen that helped Liverpool to European glory, (from left to right) Graeme Souness, Kenny Dalglish, and Alan Hansen

Hansen his international bow against Wales in 1979, but only 25 caps would follow over the next eight years. Of those, Stein selected him on 23 occasions before his sudden death meant Alex Ferguson taking temporary charge of the national team for the World Cup finals in Mexico. Ferguson opted not to take Hansen at all – an unpopular and highly contentious decision that also convinced Kenny Dalglish to quit international football. Andy Roxburgh took over after the World Cup and selected Hansen three more times in 1987, his last cap being against the Republic of Ireland in 1987. Hansen retired from playing in 1990, steadfastly maintaining he had no interest in moving into club management and despite several offers, he went on to become one of the most respected pundits on national TV. His lack of recognition for Scotland, as Hansen himself might put it, remains "unbelievable!"

Hartford, Asa
(1972 – 82)

ASA HARTFORD WAS AN INTEGRAL part of the national team for a decade and entered the Hall of Fame when he won his 50th – and final – cap against Brazil in 1982. Born in Clydebank in 1950, Hartford began his professional career in 1967 with West Bromwich Albion and his mix of silk and steel in the Baggies' dressing room seemed to have won him a dream move to Don Revie's Leeds United in November 1971. There, Hartford would have linked up in midfield with fellow Scot Billy Bremner, but a medical revealed Asa had a hole in his heart and the deal collapsed. Despite Hartford's obvious health, the Elland Road club saw the deal as a risk and though both Revie and the player were said to be devastated, Hartford got back to business on the field and, if anything, showed even greater determination to succeed. He was rewarded with a first Scotland cap in 1972 against Peru and as he established himself in the national team, his dream of playing for a top club in England was realised with a £250,000 move to Manchester City. At Maine Road, Hartford proved a huge hit with the supporters and, during that time, a Scotland team without the industrious midfield playmaker seemed unthinkable. He played in all three of Scotland's ill-fated World Cup matches in Argentina and, in 1981, captained his country for the first time, wearing the armband twice more before his final appearance against Brazil in 1982.

Player stats:

Caps   0
Goals   5

LEFT Asa Hartford in His 1978 World Cup Kit

Hendry, Colin

(1993 – 2001)

Player stats:

Caps: 51
Goals: 3

RIGHT Colin Hendry
FAR RIGHT Parkhead, home to Celtic

CONSIDERING HE WAS SOMETHING of a late starter on the international scene, Colin Hendry packed an awful lot into to his eight years with Scotland. A whole-hearted team player, Hendry began his career largely as a striker and played up front for Dundee for four years before joining Blackburn Rovers where he was converted to central defence. After two successful seasons at Ewood Park, where he netted at a rate better than one every five games, he joined Manchester City for £700,000 and was an instant hit with the City fans who adored his passion, commitment and bombarding runs forward. After picking up the Player of the Year award in his first season, Peter Reid replaced Howard Kendall as manager and shortly after Hendry was on his way back to Blackburn. In 1993, he won his first Scotland cap at the ripe old age of 27 during a 3-0 win over Estonia and in May 1996, he became Scotland captain for the first time against the USA.

He would skipper his country a further 21 times, the final occasion being against San Marino in 2001, memorably marked by two goals and a six-match ban for elbowing an opponent! At 36, that effectively ruled him out of international football and his retirement from club football followed shortly after. Hendry was installed as manager of Clyde in 2007.

Home Grounds

SCOTLAND HAVE PLAYED INTERnational home games at 18 different venues during their history with, no surprises, the third and current Hampden Park easily topping the list.

Parkhead, Ibrox, the original Hampden Park and Pittodrie have all hosted 10 or more.

The full list is, in order of most games hosted:

Stadium:
Hampden Park (current)
Parkhead
Ibrox
Hampden Park (1st)Pittodrie
Tynecastle
Easter Road
Rugby Park
West of Scotland Cricket Ground
Dens Park
Cathkin Park
Hampden Park (2nd)
Cappielow Park
Carolina Port
Fir Park

Home Internationals

THE BRITISH HOME CHAMPION-ship, popularly known as 'The Home Internationals' was conceived in the late 1800s after the Scottish, English, Welsh and Irish Football Associations formed the International Football Association Board (IFAB) in 1882. The four countries met for regular friendlies up to that point, though each association had its own rules and regulations. The IFAB agreed one set of rules for all four nations and the annual British Home Championships were born, with the first match played on January 24, 1884 between Ireland and Scotland. In what was the world's first international tournament Scotland won 5-0 and went on to lift the trophy – and successfully defend it for the next three years. England and Scotland dominated the competition for the first 22 years and the championships were eagerly awaited by each nation for more than 70 years. Playing to packed houses for the right to be crowned British champions, the Scottish and English domination con-

tinued and in 1950, Ireland became a republic and Northern Ireland continued to compete as part of the British Isles. The emergence of the World Cup and, later, the European Championships somewhat diluted the importance of the Home Internationals (though in 1950 & 1954 they doubled up as World Cup qualifying groups) and gradually the tournament began to die a slow death. Finally, in 1984, following Scotland's and then England's withdrawal from the planned 1985 competition, it ceased all together. It had lasted exactly 100 years and Scotland won the trophy 41 times (17 of which were shared). Ironically, Scotland had finished first and Ireland last in the first championship, but for the last, Northern Ireland topped the group and Scotland finished last!

ABOVE The crowd behind one of the goals during a match between England and Scotland

LEFT The stunning Ibrox in all its glory

Iran

WORLD CUP GROUP 4, June 7, 1978 – the date of Scotland's one and only game against Iran is memorable because of only one reason – the failure to beat the Middle Eastern minnows. Andy Gray, in one of his earliest punditry roles, confidently predicted Scotland would erase the 3-1 defeat to Peru and score "four or five goals" against the Iranians. Nothing less than a win would satisfy the already-furious Tartan Army and manager Ally MacLeod knew his neck was on the line prior to kick off. The tension showed during the first half, with Scotland finding it difficult to unlock Iran's defence and it wasn't until the 44th minute that the Scots broke through – and even then it was courtesy of an Andaranik Eskandarian own goal. With less than 8,000 watching the game, Iran fought back with an equaliser from Iraj Danaifar just past the hour-mark. From there on the game could have gone either way, but eventually ended without further scoring. One point from a possible four and a miracle required against Holland, the travelling Scotland fans demanded their money back in no uncertain terms. Unsurprisingly, Scotland have never elected to play a friendly against Iran since and this match remains the one and only fixture.

Italy

THOUGH SCOTLAND'S RECORD against Italy doesn't look very impressive on paper, going into the do-or-die European Championship decider at Hampden Park in November 2007, there was cause for optimism because the only three games Italy had failed to win in this fixture had all been on Scottish soil. A point would ultimately have been good enough to send Alex McLeish's side to the championships in Switzerland and Austria, and for 89 minutes it seemed like that was exactly what the hosts would earn. Of course, due to an incredibly poor refereeing decision, Italy scored a gut-wrenching last-minute winner to dump Scotland out of the tournament, despite a magnificent qualifying campaign. There is a happier memory from previous years and it came in the form of an 88th minute Scottish winner, when John Grieg scored the only goal of a 1965 World Cup qualifier in front of 101,393 delirious Hampden Park fans. Led by Jim Baxter, it was a famous and

ABOVE Franco Baresi is closed down by Stuart McCall during the World Cup qualifier, 1993

deserved win against the Azzuri, who had a tremendous side at the time, though Italy gained revenge in the return match in Rome, triumphing 3-0 in Naples on their way to qualification for England '66.

Johnston, Mo
(1984 – 91)

THERE IS SOMETHING ABOUT THE surname Johnston, whether spelled with or without an 'e' at the end. Following in the footsteps of Jimmy Johnstone and Willie Johnston, Mo Johnston's career was plagued by controversy, though almost entirely at club level in this particular instance. A rare beast indeed, Mo Johnston was a natural goalscorer and therefore coveted by both club and country. Glasgow-born Johnston made his name with Partick Thistle and won his first cap in 1984 against Wales, aged 20, scoring in a 2-1 win. A subsequent move south to Watford followed prior to Johnston becoming a huge crowd favourite with Celtic during the mid-Eighties, before moving on to French side Nantes for two years. Despite claiming he wouldn't return to Scottish club football, he seemed set for an emotional return to Parkhead in 1989 – only to sign for arch-enemy Rangers in one of the most dramatic transfer twists in SPL history.

Despite the vilification from Celtic supporters, he continued to score regularly for his country and his six-goal haul was key to qualification for the 1990 World Cup. His last international goal was during the 1990 World Cup – a penalty against Sweden – taking his tally to a respectable 14 goals, and he would play just twice more for his country.

ABOVE Mo Johnston celebrates after scoring a penalty during the World Cup match against Sweden, 1990

Player stats:	
Caps	38
Goals	14

Johnston, Willie (1965 – 78)

RIGHT Fiery Willie Johnston

CONTROVERSY IS A WORD OFTEN associated with fiery Scotland winger Willie Johnston and it is perhaps his numerous brushes with authorities that cost the talented winger more caps for his country – he won just 21 in 13 years of service for the national team. Beginning his career with Rangers, he won his first cap aged 18 during a 2-1 defeat to Poland, but he will forever be associated with two incidents involving Argentina. The first was while playing the South Americans, with Johnston, by then a West Bromwich Albion player, sent for an early bath following two bookable fouls. Almost exactly a year later, he tested positive to banned substances during Scotland's ill-fated World Cup campiagn in Argentina. Following a 3-1 defeat to Peru, Johnston was sent home in disgrace and would never play for Scotland again – his club career thereafter began to peter out somewhat disappointingly, and he moved across the Atlantic to play for Vancouver Whitecaps for a while. He

never scored for his country and with the talent he undoubtedly had, should have won perhaps double the amount caps he actually did.

Johnstone, Jimmy (1964 – 74)

JIMMY 'JINKY' JOHNSTONE IS ONE of Scottish football's favourite sons, though surprisingly he only won 23 caps during a decade of involvement with the national team. Born in Viewpark, North Lanarkshire in 1944, Jinky was scouted by Celtic and Manchester United aged only 13, though it was the Glasgow giants he opted for, beginning a 13-year love affair with the Parkhead supporters who, almost 30 years later, would vote him their greatest player of all time.

A wonderfully talented winger, he was a box of tricks and a delight to watch at club level and it was no surprise when he won his first cap for Scotland just three days after his 21st birthday – a 3-2 defeat to Wales. It was expected to be the first of an avalanche of appearances for his country, but it proved anything but. He actually won six caps during his final year with the national side in 1974, still only aged 30. Of the four goals he scored, two were against England, and arguably his best ever performance for Scotland came

Player stats:

Caps 23
Goals 4

LEFT Jimmy Johnstone, famed for his speed and immaculate control

in May 1974 during a 2-0 win over England. England skipper Emlyn Hughes was given a torrid afternoon by Jinky, leaving Hughes to comment later, "I was embarrassed to come off the pitch. Jimmy Johnstone absolutely crucified me. Alf Ramsey came up and said 'you've just played against a world-class player today. He can do that to anybody'".

He won his final cap just seven months later as part of the Scottish team that lost 2-1 to Spain. A legendary figure and one of the most gifted Scotland players ever, Jinky was diagnosed with motor neurone disease in November 2001 and finally lost his battle against the illness on March 13, 2006.

Jordan, Joe (1964 – 74)

Player stats:

Caps   52
Goals   11

RIGHT Joe Jordan in action for Scotland, 1978

A MEMBER OF THE SCOTLAND Hall of Fame, Joe Jordan served his country with pride for almost a decade, and his famous toothless snarl (he had four front teeth knocked out while playing for Leeds) was enough to make any defender wish they were elsewhere for 90 minutes! A fearsome physical presence, there have been few better headers of the ball than Jordan over the years and despite his relatively poor return of 11 goals in 52 appearances, his assists number many more and he was equally happy to be part of a goal as much scoring one himself. He began life with Morton before transferring to Leeds United and becoming a legend at Elland Road and then again at Manchester United. He made his debut for Scotland aged 20, coming on as a 70th minute replacement for Lou Macari during a Home International defeat to England, but the young forward would do enough to impress national team manager Willie Ormond and was included in the 1974 squad travelling to the World Cup in West Germany. He would play all three games at the tournament,

ABOVE Joe Jordan playing for his country against England at Wembley, 1979

scoring a last-minute equaliser against Yugoslavia. He continued to lead the line throughout the mid-Seventies and played a dramatic role in ensuring Scotland qualified for the 1978 World Cup finals, winning a late penalty in a play-off with Wales at Liverpool's Anfield. Jordan went up for a cross and the ball hit his arm, but the referee thought it had hit a Welsh arm and awarded a penalty which was successfully converted by Don Masson. Jordan took part in all three of Scotland's 1978 World Cup matches in Argentina, scoring against Peru in the opening game. He won his 50th cap against Wales in 1982 and became the first Scotland player to score in three different World Cup finals, scoring against the USSR before injury forced him off the field – his last appearance for the national team. Few forwards have given more or served their country with greater distinction – or aggression – than Joe Jordan.

Kilt

RIGHT Scotland fan in good mood prior to the start of the World Cup qualifying match against Estonia, 1997

NO SELF-RESPECTING MEMber of the Tartan Army would even consider following Scotland abroad without donning a kilt. Universally recognised as the symbol of any proud Scotsman, the kilted supporter is also recognised across Europe and the world as an ambassador for his country, and more often than not represents more peaceful invasions than many of the ancestral kilt-wearers took part in! Must-have additional clothing to the kilt includes a Balmoral hat, plus clansman badge, sporran, sgian dubh (sharp knife for those unfamiliar with Scottish traditional dress code!) which is kept at the top of the kilt hose (socks), though prohibited from most stadiums and airports around the globe for obvious reasons. Gillie Brogues are the correct footwear for any kilt-wearer, though the Argyll jacket, shirt and tie are often substituted for white t-shirts, particularly in hot countries. If you're after a touch of stereotyping, just add a few cans of Skol and Irn Bru and you've got the perfect away kit!

Law, Denis (1958 – 74)

IT IS NOT ONLY MANCHESTER United fans who refer to Denis Law as 'The King' – supporters in Scotland hold the legendary striker with equal reverence thanks to his incredible record at international level during a 16-year period. Law's 30-goal haul in just 55 appearances speaks for itself, and it's fitting that another iconic Scotland star, Kenny Dalglish, is the only man to equal Law's scoring record, though he took almost double the amount of caps to achieve the feat.

Born in February 1940 the Aberdeen-raised Law would spend his entire career playing club football outside of Scotland, signing for Huddersfield Town as a 16-year-old schoolboy in 1955. It was while he was with the Terriers that he was awarded his first Scotland cap aged 18, and the skinny teenager, one of the youngest debutants

Player stats:

Caps 55
Goals 30

LEFT England goalkeeper Ron Springett leaps to take the ball with Scotland forward Denis Law challenging

LAW

of modern times, duly bagged a goal in a 3-0 win over Wales. It was the beginning of a spectacular career that would see the youngster go on to incredible highs and break numerous records for club and country.

Indeed, his scoring exploits led to a British transfer record when Manchester City took him from West Yorkshire to Maine Road for £55,000 – £10,000 more than the previous landmark fee – and Law was soon scoring goals for fun for City, including a double hat-trick against Luton Town in the FA Cup – a game that was abandoned with still more than 20 minutes to go! He continued to collect caps for Scotland despite moving to Italy for another transfer record, with Torino splashing out £125,000 for his services in 1961. The move abroad lasted just a year, with Law returning to Manchester to play his club football – only this time, the destination was Old Trafford – and so began a love affair between player and United supporters that lasted for more than a decade.

Law skippered Scotland for the first time aged 24, during a 1-0 defeat to the Republic of Ireland in 1963, and would go on to lead his country four more times, but it was his 16 goals in nine appearances between November 1962

and May 1963 that etched the predatory Law into Scotland folklore. He twice bagged four goals and also scored a hat-trick during the most prolific spell of goals in the history of Scottish international football. It was nothing short of incredible, and though he would never quite reach those heights again, his reputation was set in stone.

Law became an integral part of Matt Busby's all-conquering Manchester United side of the late Sixties and though he missed the 1968 European Cup final through injury, he collected numerous domestic winner's medals with the Reds.

Surprisingly, Law was allowed to leave Old Trafford in 1973 and returned for one last hurrah with Manchester City. His last game in league football saw his clever back-heel condemn United to a 1-0 defeat – and certain relegation – at Old Trafford and in one of football's ultimate ironies, he then traipsed off the pitch, inconsolable. Though he would never play club football again, the 34-year-old Law played one last time for Scotland in the 1974 World Cup, playing the entire 90 minutes during a 2-0 win over Zaire, finally bringing down the curtain on a magnificent career.

ABOVE Jim Leighton shouting orders to his team

RIGHT Jim Leighton, perhaps the greatest Scottish keeper ever

Leighton, Jim (1982 – 98)

Jim Leighton's portrait hangs proudly in Scotland's Hall of Fame and who would argue that he isn't the greatest Scottish goalkeeper of all time? With 91 caps earned during a 16-year stint as the largely undisputed international No 1, Leighton played for his country up until his 40th birthday and is the second highest cap-winner in Scotland's history. He began as he meant to go on, with a clean sheet back in October 1982 against East Germany.

The Johnstone-born shot-stopper became an Aberdeen legend, playing 300 times for the Pittodrie side during a glorious 10-year spell, in which he collected nine winner's medals (including two SPL titles) before following his former manager Alex Ferguson to Manchester United for three, largely unsuccessful years. His renaissance began with a return North of the Border and he played for Dundee and Hibs before, fittingly, ending his career where it had all began, at Aberdeen. The only serious challenger to his throne was Andy Goram, who finally edged the battle for the Scotland jersey in the early nineties. At a time when Scottish goalkeepers were the butt of numerous jokes, Leighton turned the tide earning the respect of England's Peter Shilton, who said: "Scotland have now solved their goalkeeeper problem." A reliable and fantastic servant for both club and country, Leighton is now the goalkeeping coach for Aberdeen.

Macleod, Ally (1977 – 78)

Match stats:

P	17
W	7
D	5
L	5
F	26
A	21 + 5

RIGHT Ally Macleod,
1978

FEW SCOTLAND MANAGERS MADE the dramatic impact Ally MacLeod did during his relatively brief reign as the national team boss. Brash and outspoken, MacLeod took his side to the 1978 World Cup in Argentina expecting nothing less than a semi-final place and, for a while, the whole country believed his dream.

After successful spells in club management with Ayr and Aberdeen, MacLeod was appointed Scotland boss in May 1977 following Willie Ormond's departure, introducing himself to the squad in typical fashion by saying, "My name is Ally MacLeod and I am a winner." He backed his statement by guiding Scotland to World Cup qualification and refused to water down an expectant nation's hopes. On the eve of the tournament, he was asked by a journalist at a packed Prestwick Airport prior to departure what his plans were after Scotland had won the World Cup? MacLeod replied: "To retain it."

The supporters loved his almost arrogant optimism and cries of "We're on the march with Ally's Army!" would follow the squad from Hampden Park to South America in anticipation of a successful campaign, particularly after MacLeod added he would return home with "at least a medal!"

Things weren't quite so rosy behind the scenes, however, with rumblings of squad discontent materialising in a dreadful opening defeat to Peru, a display MacLeod claimed bluntly was "rank bad." Disputes over bonuses surfaced as well as boredom and poor organisation, all of which compounded team morale. Worse still, Willie Johnstone was sent home in disgrace for taking a banned substance after failing a urine test. At a press conference, the by now beleaguered Scotland manager saw a mongrel dog approach and said: "I think he is the only friend I have got left," and stretched out a hand. The urban myth that the dog bit him, is false, though it would have been better than the dog's abuse he was about to get from the Tartan Army, who demanded their money back following another lacklustre display, this time against Iran, in the next match.

With the pressure clearly showing on MacLeod, he was given a stay of execution as his side produced a stunning 3-2 victory over Holland, though it was too little, too late and Scotland were dumped out of the competition. Realising he would never shrug off the events that preceded the victory over the Dutch, MacLeod presided over one more game before tendering his resignation.

Later, he admitted that he wondered whether he had probably "generated too much excitement," prior to the World Cup. Forever associated with the negatives of Argentina, Macleod said philosophically, "I am a very good manager who just happened to have a few disastrous days, once upon a time, in Argentina."

Malpas, Maurice (1984-92)

Player stats:

Caps 55
Goals 0

RIGHT Maurice Malpas is tackled by Ray Wilkins of England during the Rous Cup match, 1985

NOT UNLIKE SCOTLAND FULL-BACK Danny McGrain, Maurice Malpas spent an entire career at one club, exceeded 50 caps without ever scoring and is one of Scottish football's most respected professionals – alas, unlike McGrain he didn't sport a permanent beard. Malpas began his 21-year career with Dundee United in 1979 and five years later he won his first cap against France. For the next eight years, Malpas's name was one of the first on the Scotland team-sheet and over the next eight years he amassed 55 caps, passing the landmark half century against Norway. He was named as skipper for that game, the second time he'd worn the skipper's armband for his country having led the team against Bulgaria two years earlier (both games ended in a draw). Malpas ended his international career against Italy in 1992, though he continued playing for Dundee United for another eight years, creating a club record with 617 appearances. Consistently good – and more often than not outstanding –

Malpas is another Scotland stalwart. He retired in 2000 moving into management and after a temporary role as Scotland Under-21 boss he joined League One side Swindon Town.

McAllister, Gary (1990-99)

GARY MCALLISTER'S SCOTLAND career ended as it began, with a single goal defeat at Hampden Park, but the elegant midfield playmaker enjoyed almost a decade in-between representing his country with the guile and grace that made him a huge favourite with the Tartan Army. After making his name with his hometown club Motherwell, McAllister moved south to join Leicester City in 1985, going on to make more than 200 appearances with the Foxes. He then moved to Leeds United, where he arguably enjoyed his best years, inspiring the Elland Road side to the league title in 1991/92 and becoming a regular in the national team, despite having to wait until the relatively late age of 25 to win his first cap. McAllister was hugely popular with the Leeds fans who were sad to see their hero go to Coventry in 1996, by which time McAllister was regularly captaining his country and was easily the most important member of the team, with most of the creativity coming from his

ABOVE Gary McAllister outjumps Paul Ince of England, 1996

cultured feet. By the time he joined Liverpool in 2000, he had won the last of his 57 caps for Scotland – injury prevented him adding to that tally and also kept him out of the 1998 World Cup in France. He rejoined Coventry in 2002, becoming player/manager at Highfield Road before resigning due to personal reasons, before resuming his managerial career with Leeds United in 2008. Quite simply, a class act on and off the pitch.

Player stats:

Caps	57
Goals	5

McCoist, Ally

(1986-98)

FOR A STRIKER WITH A PROLIFIC scoring record at club level, Ally McCoist never quite transferred that form to the international stage. His 19 goals in 61 starts is a ratio of almost a goal every three games and places him in fifth position of all-time goalscorers, but McCoist's strike rate for Rangers, where he would spend a total of 15 years, is nothing short of superb. Having initially made his name with St Johnstone, the North Lanarkshire youngster moved to Sunderland in 1981, aged 19, spending two years in a struggling Roker Park side. Rangers, who initially lost out to Sunderland for McCoist, returned for him in 1983 – one of the best pieces of business the Ibrox side ever made. He scored 251 goals in 483 SPL games for Rangers, winning nine titles and numerous trophies before ending his time with the Gers and playing out his career with Kilmarnock. He made his debut for Scotland against Holland in 1986, captaining the team for his 50th cap against Australia and his final international appearance was during a 3-2 win over Belarus in October, 1998. McCoist enjoyed a decade of success on various TV shows and spent 11 years as a captain on the BBC's A Question of Sport. In 2004 he became part of Scotland manager Walter Smith's coaching staff and in 2007 he again joined Smith, this time as Assistant Manager at Rangers.

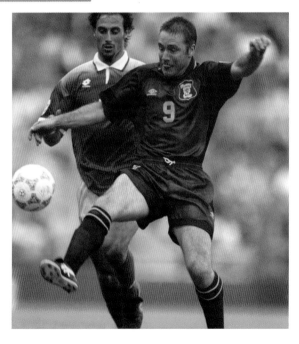

McColl, Robert

(1896-1908)

ROBERT SMITH MCCOLL'S 13 CAPS may not be world shattering in the grand scheme of Scottish football, but the prolific striker's career is worthy of note, all the same. He played international football over a 12-year period – an average of slightly better than one cap per season – but when he played for his country, he invariably grabbed the headlines thanks to his magnificent record of three hat-tricks in just five appearances which is unlikely to ever be bettered. In a golden age of Scottish football, McColl was only on the losing side once during his 13 starts and he played his club football for Queen's Park, Newcastle United and Rangers. Good to the last, he scored six goals in his final appearance for Queen's Park against Port Glasgow Athletic – a record that still stands more than 100 years on. McColl ensured his name would enjoy the kind of longevity even players with far higher profiles could ever imagine when he lent his name to the newspaper chain he set up with his brother Tom in 1901. Earning him the nickname 'Toffee Bob', the RS McColl business ensured a comfortable retirement from football and he lived to the grand old age of 83.

Player stats:

Caps	13
Goals	13

LEFT Bob McColl played for Newcastle United

FAR LEFT Ally McCoist of Scotland in action during the Euro 96

McFadden, James (2002-present)

JAMES MCFADDEN UNDOUBTEDLY has what it takes to become a true Scotland great. Blessed with a rare ability to effortlessly take his club form into the international arena, McFadden is well on his way to a half century of caps and will most likely achieve the feat before his 26th birthday, making him a potential candidate to one day perhaps even top Kenny Dalglish's 102 cap record. Not only that, but McFadden could well top Dalglish's and Denis Law's record of 30 goals for Scotland – going into 2008 he was already almost halfway there with 13. Of those strikes, none is more famous than the 25-yard screamer in Paris that gave Scotland a memorable 1-0 win over France in 2007 but that was just one of several terrific strikes McFadden has managed during his international career. The former Motherwell star, voted Scottish Young Player of the Year in 2002/03, made his name with Everton, making more than 100 appearances for the Goodison Park club, though he left for Birmingham City at the start of 2008. An explosive talent and a matchwinner in his day, the Scotland Hall of Fame beckons for the Glasgow-born forward.

ABOVE James McFadden clashes with Holland's Andre Ooijer during the Euro 2004 qualifying match

Player stats:

Caps 37
Goals 13

McGrain, Danny (1973-82)

PARKHEAD LEGEND DANNY MC-Grain, a boyhood Rangers fan, was famously snubbed by his heroes as a schoolboy when a scout mistakenly assumed his surname meant his was Catholic. Celtic took on the young defender and so began one of football's greatest associations, with McGrain going on to become one of the Bhoys' all-time greats, making 657 appearances over a 17-year period. McGrain would make a disappointing start for his country with his first three appearances during the 1973 Home Internationals ending in defeat – worse still, McGrain was diagnosed with diabetes shortly after. But McGrain, tough as old boots, was not about to let the condition stop him playing the game he

ABOVE Captain Danny McGrain leads his team out before a match against England

McGRAIN

FAR RIGHT Alex McLeish in his role as Scotland Manager

BELOW Gary Lineker is challenged by Alex McLeish during the Rous Cup Match at Wembley, 1988

loved and, able to control his blood sugars, he continued his career as though nothing was wrong. McGrain would captain his country on 10 occasions, six of which ended in victory and during the six games he played at the World Cup finals, he was never on the losing side. Many claimed McGrain's absence through injury at the 1978 World Cup cost Scotland the chance to progress and after nearly a decade of representing his country, he won his 62nd and final cap against the USSR in 1982.

McLeish, Alex

(1980-93 and Manager 2007)

FOR HIS SUCCESS AS A PLAYER AND for his impressive, but all too brief reign as Scotland manager, Alex McLeish must be considered as one of Scotland's greatest servants. The flame-haired centre-back forged an excellent partnership with Willie Miller, first with Aberdeen, then at international level, with the pair rarely playing apart for the best part of a decade. Renfrewshire-born McLeish, nicknamed 'Big Eck', joined Aberdeen in 1976 aged 17 and within two years, was a first-team regular. Under the stewardship of Alex Ferguson, McLeish enjoyed great success with the Dons and it was no surprise when he was awarded his first cap against Portugal in March 1980, playing alongside Liverpool stalwart Alan Hansen. Throughout the decade, McLeish and Miller were the spine of the national team and McLeish would earn a total of 77 caps, though he never found the net in any of them. After a two-year absence from the international stage, he returned to captain Scotland for the last time (he'd skippered the team on seven previous occasions) during a 3-0 win over Malta. After 16 years at Pittodrie and 493 league games, he left to join Motherwell as player/manager in 1994, making just three appearances before retiring to fully concentrate on management. McLeish would enjoy reasonable success with the 'Well, then Hibs, before taking the Rangers job and guiding the Ibrox side to great success.

In 2007, he succeeded Walter Smith as Scotland boss and almost guided Scotland to the 2008 European Championships, despite being in a group that contained France and World Champions Italy, and only a controversial last-minute winner by the Italians in the final game denied qualification. In November 2007, just 11 months after taking on the role of national team boss, McLeish quit to join Birmingham City, despite, statistically, the best record of any Scotland manager – ever.

Manager stats:

P	10
W	7
D	0
L	3
F	14
A	9 + 5

Player stats:

Caps	77
Goals	0

RIGHT Paul McStay in
Action against England

McStay, Paul (1983-1997)

NICKNAMED 'THE MAESTRO' BY the Celtic fans who adored him, Paul McStay added a touch of culture and more than a dash of class during his distinguished career for both club and country. Like so many true Scotland greats, McStay was a one-club man and he joined the Parkhead club in 1981, aged 17. He scored on his Celtic debut in 1982 and he quickly established a reputation as one of Scottish football's hottest properties, captaining his country at Under-18 level to European Championship glory that same year. His progression to the senior Scotland squad was merely a matter of time and a year later he won his first full cap in a 2-0 win over Uruguay. It was the first of 77 appearances for his country over a 14-year period and during all that period, he played exclusively for Celtic – not that there wasn't plenty of interest from numerous top English clubs over the years. McStay sits proudly in fourth position in the list of Scotland cap-winners – his last international start was in April 1997 against Austria – and he finished just one appearance behind Alex McLeish. After more than 500 appearances for the Bhoys, he retired in 1997.

Miller, Kenny (2001-present)

NOT UNLIKE JAMES MCFADDEN, Kenny Miller should take his place in the Scotland Hall of Fame within the next few years as a half century of caps quickly approaches. Something of a nomadic player at club level, the Edinburgh-born striker has played for six different teams, including Hibs, Rangers, Celtic, Wolves and Derby County – the latter being his current home. After picking up the Scottish Young Player of the Year award in 2000 while with Hibs, Miller moved on to Rangers for £2m and towards the end of his first season at Ibrox, he made his international debut against Poland. He has been a regular for his country since then, sometimes playing as part of a front pairing, sometimes as a lone striker. His energetic, wholehearted attitude has ensured he has retained his place under three different Scotland managers and his 10-goal haul represents a decent return from his 35 caps. He has been booked in four internationals – and scored in each game where he was cautioned – clearly, the passion burns brightly for Miller every time he pulls on the navy blue jersey.

BELOW Kenny Miller celebrates after scoring against Ukraine

Player stats:

Caps 35
Goals 10

Miller, Willie (1975-89)

RIGHT Willie Miller in action during a World Cup qualifying match against Spain, 1985

WILLIAM FERGUSON MILLER WAS born in Glasgow on May 2, 1955 and would go on to become one of Scotland's greatest players. Miller joined Aberdeen aged 16 and would only ever play his club football for the Dons, despite plenty of interest from teams both north and south of the border. Steady as a rock and rarely injured, he would amass more than 800 appearances and forged a formidable partnership with Alex McLeish at Pittodrie. Miller was awarded his first cap aged 20, though it would be another three years before he next played for his country. He then retained his place for the best part of a decade and it was during his last appearance for his country – a 1-1 draw with Norway in 1989 – that he suffered an injury that eventually forced him to retire. He captained Aberdeen for many years and led Scotland on 11 occasions before hanging his boots up in 1990. In 1992, he became Aberdeen boss after enjoying a spell as coach at Pittodrie. The Dons twice finished SPL runners-up under his tenure – not to mention two cup final appearances but despite his legendary status and success with the club and its supporters, he was sacked in 1995, though his place in the Scotland Hall of Fame is assured.

O'Donnell (1993)

ONE OF THE MOST RESPECTED players in modern Scottish football, Phil O'Donnell was desperately unlucky to have had just – literally – 15 minutes of fame when it came to international football. The Motherwell legend came on as a 75th minute substitute for Dave Bowman in the 1-1 draw with Switzerland in 1993 and never played for his country again. Though aged only 21 at the time, he inexplicably slipped beneath the radar of a succession of national team managers, despite winning eight Under-21 caps and winning the Scottish PFA Young Player of the Year award in both 1992 and 1994. After four years at the 'Well, he joined Celtic for a club record £1.75m, but was plagued with numerous injuries throughout his Parkhead career. A move to Sheffield Wednesday resulted in just 20 appearances in four years and he was given a free transfer in 2003, but when some thought O'Donnell's days in top flight football might be numbered, Motherwell invited him to train with them and were impressed enough to re-sign him in January 2004. After just a year back at Fir Park, he was made Captain and still wore the armband up until his tragic death in December 2007. O'Donnell collapsed as he was about to be substituted during an SPL clash with Dundee United and despite desperate efforts to revive him, he passed away shortly after of heart failure, leaving a wife and four young children. O'Donnell was described as "the perfect gentleman" by former Scotland boss Craig Brown and the touching tributes from the world of football following his death gave some solace to his grieving family.

ABOVE Phil O'Donnell (left) and Ian Angus (right) of Motherwell celebrate a second goal during the Scottish Cup final against Dundee

Player stats:

| Caps | 1 |
| Goals | 0 |

Ormond, Willie

(1954 – 59 & Manager 1973-77)

Manager stats:	
P	38
W	18
D	8
L	12
F	55
A	39 + 16

Player stats:	
Gaps	6
Goals	2

FORMER SCOTLAND INTERNATIONAL Willie Ormond certainly knew how to heap pressure upon himself and earn the anger of a nation when, as newly appointed Scotland boss, his first game ended in a 5-0 home defeat to England! Fortunately, he survived any early calls for his head and went on to become one of the national team's longest-serving managers and even managed a World Cup tournament along the way. Ormond made one of the worst starts of any Scotland manager when he tasted defeat eight times in his first 11 games, but by the time he left the post in 1977, Scotland had won 10 of their previous 11 games – quite a turn around and proof that he had been the right man for the job after all.

At the 1974 World Cup, Ormond's side were forced to return home early after the first round of games, despite being unbeaten in all three group matches. Uniquely, Scotland would be the only side not to lose a single game at the '74 World Cup. Despite his relative success, the SFA decided they wanted a tougher disciplinarian and a more charismatic figure to lead them through the next World Cup qualifiers and Ormond left his post in May 1977.

Peru

THOUGH SCOTLAND AND PERU have met only three times, the South Americans will be forever etched into the memories of every Scotsman old enough to remember the 1978 World Cup. Prior to the meeting in Argentina, Scotland had beaten Peru 2-0 in a friendly at Hampden Park with goals from Denis Law and John O'Hare in 1972. Understandably, Scotland were strong favourites to beat the Peruvians when the teams met again in the opening World Cup Group D match in '78. Things seemed to be going according to plan when Joe Jordan scored after just 15 minutes, but Cesar Cueto levelled the scores just before the break and the Scots' nerves began to jangle. A draw wouldn't have been a disaster, but two strikes from Teofilio Cubillas on 72 and 77 minutes secured a famous victory for Peru and shattered Scotland's confidence. It was a

bitter pill to swallow. Eager to exorcise the memory of the Cordoba loss, a friendly was arranged at Hampden Park a year later, but despite Jorge Olaechea's own goal after four minutes, Peru levelled after the break through German Leguia to take a creditable draw. The spectre of Teofilio Cubillas still hangs over Scottish football to this day…

Match stats:	
P	3
W	1
D	1
L	1
F	4
A	4

Play-Offs

Match stats:

P	7
W	3
D	1
L	3
F	6
A	12

SCOTLAND HAVE BEEN INVOLVED IN four World Cup and European Championships play-offs to date and have been successful on just one occasion. The first tie-breaker was back in 1961, when Scotland met Czechoslovakia on neutral territory (Heysel Stadium, Belgium) for the right to take part in the 1962 World Cup, but the Czech side ran out 4-2 winners. It would be 24 years before the next play-off, again for a place in the World Cup finals, with Scotland facing Australia – a first-ever meeting between the countries – over two legs. Two goals in two minutes from Frank McAvennie and David Speedie gave Alex Ferguson's side a 2-0 advantage at Hampden, and a 0-0 draw in Sydney secured passage to the 1986 World Cup in Mexico. Perhaps the most painful play-off defeat was against England in 1999 for a place at the 2000 European Championships. England won the first leg at Hampden Park 2-0, leaving the Scots with a mountain to climb, but Craig Brown's men gave a brave performance in the return leg at Wembley, winning 1-0 with a goal from Don Hutchison, though it wasn't enough. Four years later and Scotland found themselves in the same position, facing tough opposition in a play-off in order to progress to a major tournament – this time the European Championships in Portugal. Bertie Vogts' side were pitted against

ABOVE Billy Dodds takes on Gareth Southgate and Paul Ince during the Euro 2000 play-offs

LEFT Kenny Dalglish is manhandled by the Australian players during World Cup play-off match

Holland over two legs, and just edged the first leg at Hampden thanks to James McFadden's solitary strike. The second leg was an unmitigated disaster, however, with the Dutch turning in a masterful display to win 6-0.

Queens Park

THE OLDEST CLUB IN SCOTTISH football and genial hosts of the national team since its inception, Queen's Park represent all that is good in football North of the Border – and perhaps around the globe. Formed in July 1867, it was Queen's Park who influenced football and its direction in Scotland more than any other, and a decision was taken at the first embryonic meeting of the club to ensure each player who played for Queen's Park would be of amateur status and would play 'for the sake of playing' – a maxim that still exists today. Queen's Park have always played their home games at Hampden Park, though the latest version is in actual fact their third venue in total, with previous Hampden Parks each time making way for a better, more modern and spacious stadium. Though the hosts rarely play in front of crowds bigger than 4,000, their southeast Glasgow home is one of UEFA's 29 five-star stadiums, with a capacity of 52,000. Uniquely run, steeped in tradition and playing the spirit of the game as it was meant to be played, Queen's Park are at the very heart of Scottish football and it is only right that the national team should play their football at their home.

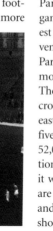

BELOW A match between Kilmarnock and Queen's Park in 1951

Red Cards

In alphabetical order, here are the bad boys – as the referees on the day saw it – each of whom were given their marching orders while representing their country:

Player & Team	Date
Billy Steel v Austria	1951
Bertie Auld v Holland	1959
Craig Burley v Morocco	1998
Matt Elliot v Faroe Islands	1999
Paddy Crerand v Czechoslovakia	1961
Tommy Gemmell v West Germany	1969
Richard Gough v Switzerland	1999
Andy Gray v Czechoslovakia	1976
Willie Johnstone v Argentina	1977
Joe Jordan v Northern Ireland	1990
John Spencer v Japan	1995
Peter Lorimer v Denmark	1972
James McFadden v Norway	2004
Steven Pressley v Ukraine	2006
Maurice Ross v Germany	2003

SCOTLAND HAVE ONE of the best disciplinary records in international football with only 15 red cards being issued over the years, up to the start of 2008. No player has been sent off more than once, though several have picked up numerous yellow cards as well (see 'Yellow Cards'). Billy Steel was the first to be sent for an early bath in 1951, though Scotland went through the 1980s without one sending off – how many other countries could claim such a pristine decade?!

ABOVE Billy Steel was infamous for being the first ever Scottish player to be sent off

Robertson, John N (1978-83)

RIGHT John Robertson who was capped 28 times

CONSIDERING HIS UNDOUBTED ability, John Robertson had a fairly brief career as a Scotland player, stretching for just five years. The Nottingham Forest winger's halcyon days for club and country were at the end of the Seventies and start of the early Eighties. He made his debut against Northern Ireland at Hampden as Ally MacLeod shaped his squad for the World Cup in Argentina and the Uddingston-born Robertson did enough to impress the new national team boss against Wales a few days later to ensure he was on the plane for Buenos Aires. Robertson had one man to thank for his promotion to the national team – Brian Clough. He'd been no more than a bit-part player at Forest until Clough arrived at the City Ground in 1975. Clough knew what made Robertson tick and for several years, he became one of the most feared forwards in English football. His only appearance at the '78 World Cup was during the 1-1 draw with Iran, but it would be the only time he took part in Scotland's ill-fated trip. In 1979 and 1980 he was a key figure in Forest's successive European Cup triumphs and he transferred that form into the national team, too, and helped his country qualify for the 1982 World Cup in Spain where he played in all three games. Wearing his beloved No 11 shirt, Robertson played his final game for Scotland against Belgium in 1983 – had Clough been his club manager sooner, he would likely have doubled his cap total.

Rough,
Alan (1976-86)

ALAN ROUGH'S 10-YEAR ASSOCIA-tion with the national team began with a clean sheet against Switzerland in April 1976. He would go on to hold the record as Scotland's most-capped keeper for almost a decade until the emergence of his successor in the national team, Jim Leighton. Rough's solid displays for Partick Thistle, where he won the majority of his caps, soon caught the eye of Scotland manager Willie Ormond and he was one of seven players to make his international debut against the Swiss. His next cap wouldn't come until five months later, but from there on, he began to establish himself as the top keeper in the country and the undisputed No 1 for the next six years, until Leighton's emergence. Fittingly, he won his 50th cap during the 1982 World Cup (Rough's second World Cup, having played all three games at Argentina '78), but had to pick the ball out of the net four times against Brazil. After the tournament, he played just twice more, once against Wales in 1985

and a year later, almost a decade to the day he made his debut, he played his last game for his country during a 2-1 Rous Cup defeat to England. A Hall of Fame member, Rough remains second only to Leighton in the list of caps won by goalkeepers.

Player stats:

Caps 53
Goals 0

BELOW Alan Rough in action for his country

Rous Cup, The

NAMED AFTER THE FORMER SECRETary of The Football Association (English) and president of FIFA, Sir Stanley Rous, The Rous Cup was, in effect, initially a replacement for the annual England v Scotland matches following the cessation of the Home International tournament a few years earlier. Scotland won the trophy in its inaugural year in 1985 with a 1-0 win at Hampden Park, but England gained revenge a year later at Wembley, winning 2-1. To add spice, a South American guest was invited for the next three years, Brazil winning the 1987 Rous Cup. England won the tournament in 1988 and again in 1989 for a third and final time before this short-lived competition was confined to history.

RIGHT Action from the Rous Cup match at Hampden Park, 1985

Team	Ground	Date	Score
Scotland v Chile	Hampden Park, Glasgow	30 May 1989	2-0
Scotland v England	Hampden Park, Glasgow	27 May 1989	0-2
England v Scotland	Wembley Stadium, London	21 May 1988	1-0
Scotland v Colombia	Hampden Park, Glasgow	17 May 1988	0-0
Scotland v Brazil	Hampden Park, Glasgow	26 May 1987	0-2
Scotland v England	Hampden Park, Glasgow	23 May 1987	0-0
England v Scotland	Wembley Stadium, London	23 April 1986	2-1
Scotland v England	Hampden Park, Glasgow	25 May 1985	1-0

Roxburgh, Andy (Manager 1986-93)

WHEN ALEX FERGUSON'S BRIEF reign as Scotland manager came to an end in 1986, the two strong favourites to take his place were Dundee United's Jim McLean and Manchester City's Billy McNeill. Both men were legendary figures within Scottish football, so it was something of a shock when the SFA's director of coaching, Andy Roxburgh, was confirmed as the new boss. Roxburgh was something of an unknown quantity to the majority of Scottish football fans, having had an unspectacular playing career with Queen's Park, Partick Thistle and Falkirk, but he made a steady start to his reign as national team boss with five points from a possible nine as Scotland began their European Championships campaign. Though Roxburgh saw his team finish second bottom of the group, they were in fact just two points behind group-winners Republic of Ireland. For the 1990 World Cup qualifiers, however, Roxburgh successfully guided his side through a tricky group that included Yugoslavia, Norway and France, though Scotland were desperately unlucky not to progress further than the group stages at Italia '90. Roxburgh again took Scotland to a major tournament – the 1992 European Championships – but again, saw his troops fall at the group stages at the finals. In 1993, after he'd equalled Jock Stein's record as longest-serving manager with 61 games and seven years under his belt, Roxburgh quit his role and was succeeded by Craig Brown. A year later he became the UEFA Technical Director – a post he still retains today.

LEFT Andy Roxburgh, 1990

Manager stats:

P	61
W	23
D	19
L	19
F	67
A	60 + 7

Same Name

Here is a list of the most common monikers:

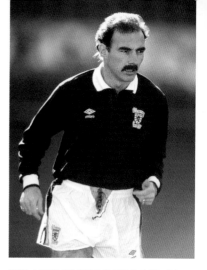

RIGHT Willie Miller who shared his name with two other players

Player Name	Use of Name
Campbell	18
Thomson	16
Smith	15
Robertson	14
Brown	14
Wilson	13
Walker	10
Hamilton	10
Miller	10
Stewart	10
Anderson	9
Baird	7
Johnstone	7
Kennedy	7
McPherson	7
Gray	7

IT'S NOT UNCOMMON FOR TWO players to have the same name and there have been 96 instances of players representing Scotland with the identical name as at least one other person. Two have cropped up more than any other with four different John McPhersons and four James Smiths having all won at least one cap. There have also been three Willie Millers, three Robert Browns, three John Camerons, three James Campbells, three David Wilsons and three James Watsons. There have also been 35 players who have shared their name with one other player. As for same surnames only, Campbell appears most often with 18 players sharing the same last name.

On the flip side, there really was only one Kenny Dalglish!

Smith, Walter

(Manager 2004-06)

WALTER SMITH'S REIGN AS SCOTland boss began and ended with a 2-0 defeat, but it was what he achieved in the 14 games in between those losses that Smith will be remembered for. Under his tenure, Scotland moved up 70 places in the FIFA World Rankings, restoring pride in the national team after his predecessor Bertie Vogts' largely disastrous time as manager. Smith had a solid club career cut short due to a pelvic injury at the age of 29, but retirement as a player led to a role as a coach at Dundee United and after showing great aptitude in his new job, he was given the task of coaching Scotland Under-18s. He guided the young Scots to success at the European Youth Championships in 1982, returning home as winners and he was then promoted to Scotland Under-21 boss. Smith's star continued to rise when he assisted Alex Ferguson at the 1986 World Cup, later become Graeme Souness' assistant at Rangers and succeeded him in 1991 – his first managerial role. After 13 trophies in seven years, including seven successive league titles, he moved to Everton, managing the Merseysiders for four years without success. He then assisted Sir Alex Ferguson again, this time at Manchester United, and remained at Old Trafford for a brief time before becoming Scotland manager in December 2004. Smith's Scotland enjoyed a run of just two defeats in 14 games, beating France at Hampden Park, and seemed to be on their way to the European Championships before strong links with the vacant manager's job at Rangers surfaced. The pull to Ibrox proved too strong for the man who had led the Gers through their most successful period ever and Smith stunned Scottish football when he resigned as national team manager to return to club football. Nobody, however, could deny he'd put his country back on the world football map again and his good work would be continued by Alex McLeish.

ABOVE Walter Smith being unvailed as the new national team Manager, 2004

Manager stats:

P	16
W	7
D	5
L	4
F	26
A	15 + 11

Songs

THERE HAVE BEEN SEVERAL WORLD Cup songs released over the years to celebrate Scotland's qualification for the finals with perhaps none more famous than 'We Have A Dream' by the Scottish World Cup Squad, which reached the Top 5 in 1982. Rod Stewart has always been an obvious candidate for Scotland songs and he's had two successes with 'Ole Ola' and 'Purple Heather'. 'Ally's Tartan Army' proved a hit for Andy Cameron prior to the 1978 World Cup and was the most successful of the four

Flower of Scotland

O flower of Scotland,
When will we see your like again,
That fought and died for,
Your wee bit hill and glen,
And stood against him,
Proud Edward's army,
And sent him homeward,
Tae think again.

The hills are bare now,
And autumn leaves lie thick and still,
O'er land that is lost now,
Which those so dearly held,
And stood against him,
Proud Edward's army,
And sent him homeward,
Tae think again.

Those days are passed now,
And in the past they must remain,
But we can still rise now,
And be the nation again,
That stood against him,
Proud Edward's army,
And sent him homeward,
Tae think again.

records he recorded over the years. As for the Tartan Army, however, the stirring anthem 'Flower of Scotland' is the song that still sends shivers down the nation's collective spine and to hear it echo around Hampden Park prior to kick-off is enough to bring a tear to the eye of any true Scotsman.

Souness, Graeme (1974-86)

RIGHT Graeme Souness in action during a World Cup qualifying match against Spain, 1985

FAR RIGHT Jock Stein, 1967

ONE OF SCOTLAND'S GREATEST servants, Graeme Souness prowled midfield for his country for a dozen years and of the 54 caps he won during that time, exactly half were as Captain. He began his career with Tottenham, but, frustrated at his lack of first-team opportunities, he joined Montreal in the NASL for the summer and on his return to England, joined Middlesbrough where his career really began to take off. Aged 21, he made his international debut in October 1974 against East Germany at Hampden, but won just a handful of caps over the next few years and it wasn't until Ally MacLeod selected him for the 1978 World Cup that Souness established himself as a regular in the national team. By now a Liverpool player, Scotland wouldn't look the same without the tough-tackling Souness marauding in the middle of the park. An inspirational player, he embodied the passion every member of the Tartan Army had on the terraces – something he believed was the minimum requirement when playing for his country. From 1982 to 1986, Souness was the Scotland Captain and his career saw him take part in three World Cups before he moved into management at Rangers, leading out the national team for the final time against West Germany in 1986.

Stein, Jock

(Manager 1965 & 1978-85)

VOTED THE GREATEST SCOTLAND manager of all time, Jock Stein is also recognised as one of the best managers in the history of British football. His achievements at Celtic are the stuff of legend and include 10 SPL titles and one European Cup success – little wonder the big man would eventually be offered the chance to manage the national team. After a solid career as a player for Albion Rovers and Celtic, he moved into management at Dunfermline before taking on the role of Hibs boss and eventually Celtic in 1965, where he would remain for 13 trophy-laden years. He also took on a caretaker role as national team boss in 1965, winning three of the seven games he took charge of before returning his full attention to the Hoops. After feeling he'd achieved all he could at Parkhead, Stein became manager of Leeds United for a couple of months before once more accepting the offer to be Scotland manager in October '78. Following the 1978 World Cup in Argentina, Stein was given the task of rebuilding a side that could win a place

at the 1982 World Cup and restoring national pride in the process. He began his reign with a European Championships qualifier against Norway, and two late goals from Kenny Dalglish and Archie Gemmill ensured he began his second spell with a victory. Though Scotland failed to make the

Manager stats:	
P	68
W	29
D	13
L	26
F	91
A	81 + 10

1980 European Championships, Stein guided them to the '82 World Cup in Spain having qualified from a tough group that included Portugal and Sweden. Despite beating New Zealand 5-2 in the first match of the '82 finals, a 4-1 defeat to Brazil was followed by a creditable 2-2 draw with the USSR – alas, it still meant an early flight home for the Stein's talented side. Again, European Championships qualification eluded Stein in 1984, but he again appeared set to lead the nation to a fourth successive World Cup when tragedy struck. Needing just a point to ensure passage to Mexico '86, Stein took his side to Ninian Park to face Wales. Mark Hughes gave the Welsh a 13th minute lead, but in the 81st minute of a nerve-wracking contest, Scotland were awarded a penalty. Davie Cooper calmly stroked home the equaliser and Scotland held onto the point they needed. Amid all the celebration, the dreadful news filtered through that Jock Stein had suffered a fatal heart attack towards the end of the match. One of Scottish football's greatest sons had gone and his last act was to guide the nation to another World Cup finals. A fitting epitaph to a great life and a great man.

Player stats:

Caps 50
Goals 5

LEFT Gordon Strachan
in action during the
1986 World Cup

Strachan, Gordon (1980-92)

GORDON STRACHAN WAS INSTANTLY recognisable in a Scotland shirt. Pint-sized, industrious with a shock of fiery red hair, Strachan made it to the 50-cap mark before calling it a day with the national team. Having made his name with Dundee in the early Seventies, Strachan moved to Aberdeen and enjoyed great success at Pittodrie under Alex Ferguson. After three years with the Dons, Strachan won his first cap against Northern Ireland. He later went on to further club successes with Manchester United, and later Leeds United, before moving to Coventry City, initially as player/coach and later player/manager. Though he was in and out of the team over the next 12 years, he served his country with distinction each time he played and was given the captain's armband on five occasions. He

ABOVE Strachan runs with the ball

RIGHT The Tartan Army celebrate a goal against England, 1977

didn't play for his country for a period of 16 months at one point, but was recalled in 1991 for a game against the USSR. Then, agonisingly edging towards his goal, he had to wait another 12 months before another recall saw him win caps 49 and 50 – he was skipper in both matches – a reward for more than a decade of loyal service. He currently manages Celtic.

Tartan Army

FOR PEOPLE WHO DON'T GET IT, the Tartan Army – Scotland's hardcore support who travel home and away decked in traditional tartans, kilts and replica Scotland jerseys – are among the most welcomed football fans anywhere in the world. The TA maxim is simple – sing, drink, support the team and be merry. Named the World's Friendliest Fans during the 1998 World Cup, there have been numerous 'invasions' over the years and any time Scotland play at Wembley, England's home becomes an extension of Hampden Park with the hosts invariably outnumbered and out-sung for the duration of the match. More than 20,000 Scots swarmed on Paris for the European Championship qualifier in 2007 but, as ever, it was a peaceful operation and regardless of results, the Tartan Army parties the night away and wins the

TARTAN ARMY

respect of the locals. Rowdy behaviour is unacceptable and often dealt with by other members of the TA and despite the fierce rivalry of Celtic and Rangers, who form the majority of the support in Scotland, all club squabbles are set aside when following the national team.

Without doubt, the most passionate and loyal supporters on the planet, the Tartan Army are a great source of inspiration and pride for the majority of Scots. Below is one of the Tartan Army's favourite songs and it sums up their attitude perfectly.

Scotland All Over the World

Ah here we are and here we are and here we go
All aboard and we're hitting the road
Here we go, Scotland all over the world

Ah giddy-up and giddy-up and get away
We're going crazy and we're going today
Here we go, Scotland all over the world

And I like it, I like it, I like it, I like it
I li-li-like it, li-li-like
Here we go, Scotland all over the world

I'm gonna tell your mama what you're gonna do
Come on out with your dancing shoes
Here we go, Scotland all over the world

And I like it, I like it, I like it, I like it
I li-li-like it, li-li-like
Here we go, Scotland all over the world

And I like it, I like it, I like it, I like it
I li-li-like it, li-li-like
Here we go, Scotland all over the world

And I like it, I like it, I like it, I like it
I li-li-like it, li-li-like
Here we go, Scotland all over the world

LEFT The Tartan Army travel all over the world to support their team

Uruguay

Match Stats:

P	4
W	1
D	1
L	2
F	4
A	10 - 6

RIGHT Richard Gough jumps for the ball during the 1986 World Cup match against Uruguay

IN 1954, SCOTLAND, PLAYING AT their first ever World Cup finals, were unfortunate to be drawn against World Champions Uruguay in the group stages of the tournament held in Switzerland. Having lost 1-0 in the opening game to Austria, Scotland – with future managers Tommy Docherty and Willie Ormond in their team – had to beat the hardy South Americans, but with the Scottish team in disarray on and off the pitch, it was no surprise that Uruguay, unbeaten in every World Cup match they'd played in up to that point, went on to record a resounding 7-0 win, sending the Scots back home at the first hurdle. While Uruguay exited at the semi-final stage, Scottish football was rocked by the humiliating defeat. It would be eight years before the SFA invited Uruguay to Hampden in an effort to exorcise the ghost of '54. In a much closer game, Scotland lost 3-2, despite a stirring comeback in front of more than 67,000 fans. It would take 29 years to finally restore some parity between the countries when, in 1983, goals from John Robertson and Davie Dodds gave Jock Stein's men a 2-0 friendly win at Hampden and the only other fixture between the sides, three years later at the Mexico World Cup in 1986, resulted in a creditable 0-0 draw.

Vogts, Berti
(Manager 2002 – 04)

WHEN SCOTLAND'S NEW MAN-ager announced at a press conference in 2002 that people should call him 'Berti McVogts', the SFA should have perhaps done the right thing and relieved him of his duties there and then. Vogts was tak-ing the place of Craig Brown, a popular and jovial character and also Scotland's longest-serving manager, so his job was never going to be easy, but his appoint-ment was greeted with a lukewarm response – at best – from the Tartan Army. What followed thereafter was one of the most miserable periods in Scotland's history. Vogts' reign began with a 5-0 defeat against France and embarrassing defeats to Nigeria, South Korea and South Africa quickly fol-lowed. The team seemed devoid of

passion and direction, but surely it was only fair to give Vogts sufficient time to bed into the job... or was it? Things went from bad to worse when Scotland's European Championship qualifiers began with what had been perceived to be a banker away win against the Faroe Islands, yet the minnows of world foot-ball were 2-0 up after just 12 minutes! The game ended 2-2, but for many Scotland fans, the die had been cast. Vogts still managed to guide his team to victories over Iceland and Lithuania, as well as take a point off Germany - enough to finish group runners-up and earn a play-off against Holland. Arguably Scotland's best performance under his reign came in the first leg against the Dutch, where James

Match stats:	
P	32
W	9
D	7
L	16
F	31
A	50 - 19

McFadden's solitary strike was enough to take a slender lead into the second leg. Holland, however, totally outclassed Scotland in the return match, racing 3-0 ahead at the break and eventually won 6-0. Many called for Vogts' head there and then, but, perhaps thinking of a hefty severance package, the SFA gave the German coach a stay of execution. It was a questionable decision to say the least, and Scotland's next game was a 4-0 humiliation by Wales. The beleaguered manager limped on for another seven months before finally leaving his post by mutual consent, citing his treatment from the Scottish tabloids and a minority of supporters as the main reasons behind his decision.

Wales

IF THE WELSH FA HAD REQUESTED an end to their annual humiliation back in the late 1800s, nobody could have blamed them. Scotland's total domination over Wales lasted almost 30 years, but by the time the Welsh finally recorded a win in 1905, the damage, statistically, had already been done.

The tone was set during the very first meeting of the two countries in 1874, with Scotland triumphing 4-0 at the West of Scotland Cricket Ground. It would be the first of 13 successive wins that saw Wales concede 59 goals and score just six. Record victories (that still stand today) were logged during that time and the 8-1 home win in 1885 and the 8-1 win in Wales in 1893, remain intact more than a century on. Wales, however, have had the better results in recent years and haven't lost against Scotland for more than 24 years, with the last clash between the two nations resulting in a 4-0 victory for the Welsh in 2004. Arguably the most memorable meeting was the 1977 World Cup qualifier at Anfield, where two late goals from Don Masson and Kenny Dalglish sent Scotland to the 1978 World Cup.

Manager stats:	
P	103
W	60
D	23
L	20
F	238
A	116 + 122

Weir, David (1997-present)

RIGHT David Weir and Bart Goor of Belgium both going for the ball during the World Cup qualiying match, 2001

FAR RIGHT The squad before the World Cup qualifyer against Sweden, 1997

ONE OF SCOTLAND'S GREATEST servants, David Weir would now probably have Kenny Dalglish's record of 102 caps won firmly in his sights – but for a fall out with former national team boss Bert Vogts. As it is, he may make the top 5 for appearances, but is unlikely to climb much higher. A solid and dependable full-back, Weir started out at club level with Falkirk before moving on to Hearts. He remained at Tynecastle for three years before joining Everton and he remained at Goodison Park for eight years before returning to the SPL with Rangers. His international debut came in 1997, when Craig Brown selected him to play against Wales. He became a permanent fixture for Scotland under Brown, but Vogts' public criticism of the player led to him retiring from international football – at least, until Vogts moved on and Walter Smith took over. After a two-year absence that perhaps cost him 20 caps or more, he returned in 2004 and resumed his Scotland career, aged 34.

In 2006, he entered the Scotland Hall of Fame by earning his 50th cap against Lithuania. He also captained the side that day and will hope to add a few more caps under new national team manager George Burley before he hangs his boots up.

World Cup

SCOTLAND HAVE QUALIFIED FOR eight World Cups, but have never progressed past the first-round phase of matches. Beginning with a 2-0 defeat against Austria in 1954, there has been little to cheer for the Tartan Army at football's most prestigious tournament – save for the odd heaven-sent moment here and there. It was 20 years before

World Cup Stats:	
P	23
W	4
D	7
L	12
F	25
A	41 - 16

Scotland's first World Cup finals win – a 2-0 victory over Zaire, but even after excellent draws against Brazil and Yugoslavia in the same group, goal difference meant another early flight home. The events of Argentina '78 are well documented in this book, but Archie Gemmill's wonder goal against Holland is always worth a mention. The 1982 finals in Spain brought more goal-difference heartache and an avalanche of goals – eight scored and eight conceded, but again it wasn't enough. The combined efforts of the 1986 and 1990 finals brought just one win in six and after five successive appearances, Scotland failed to qualify for the 1994 World Cup in the USA.

France '98 pitted Scotland against Brazil for an incredible fourth time, but despite a brave display, the silky-skilled South Americans triumphed 2-1 and failure to beat Norway and Morocco in the following games meant that, yet again, the Tartan Army's trip overseas was cut short. Scotland failed to make the finals at all in 2002 and 2006 – let's hope George Burley can guide the boys to the 2010 tournament in South Africa.

Yellow Cards

Player	Cards
Christian Dailly	12
Gary Caldwell	9
Barry Ferguson	8
James McFadden	8
Steven Pressley	7
Don Hutchison	6
Joe Jordan	6
Gary Naysmith	6
Colin Calderwood	5
John Collins	5
Darren Fletcher	5
Lee McCulloch	5
Callum Davidson	4
Paul Dickov	4
Darren Jackson	4
Kenny Miller	4
Stuart McCall	4
Graeme Souness	4

RIGHT IS A LIST OF THE PLAYERS booked most often while playing for Scotland, up to 01/02/08:

With one red card and eight yellows, the player with the worst disciplinary record for Scotland is Birmingham City's James McFadden.

LEFT James McFadden has recieved criticism for picking up more red and yellow cards than any other Scottish Player

FAR LEFT Alex McLeish and Willie Miller beat Fransisco Clos of Spain to the ball during a World Cup match

Young, George (1946-57)

THERE HAVE BEEN GIANTS OF SCOTtish football over the years, but none have eclipsed the man-mountain that was George Young, a six foot, two inch tall centre-back who it seemed was, like Irn Bru, made of girders – and equally as popular! His era for the national team was post-war and he made his debut in 1946, wearing the No 2 jersey and playing at full-back. Though not his natural position, he played there for a time for club and country to accommodate Rangers team-mate Willie Woodburn, before later moving back to central defence on the international stage and becoming Captain for Scotland for a decade. He would skipper the team for a record 48 times and become the first player to enter the Hall of Fame after earning 50 caps for Scotland, eventually earning 53 in total, though he never found the back of the net.

A Rangers legend, Young was a one-club man and was an integral part of a defence at Ibrox known as the 'Iron Curtain'. He stayed with the Ger's for 18 years, all told. Nicknamed 'Corky' because of a lucky champagne cork he carried around with him, Young made 34 consecutive Scotland appearances,

LEFT George Young and Billy Wright leading out their respective national teams

but injury cost him a place at the 1954 World Cup finals. Controversially, he wasn't selected for the 1958 World Cup – despite leading them to the finals with victories in his last two games. He moved into management at Third Lanark for three years before later becoming a hotelier. A Scotland and Rangers legend in every sense of the world, Young died aged 74 in 1997.

Zaire

ZAIRE WILL FOREVER HOLD A SPE-cial place in Scotland's history. The two countries have met just once, at the 1974 World Cup in Germany, during the first round of group matches. With difficult games against Brazil and Yugoslavia to come, Scotland had to beat the African minnows to have any chance of progressing to the second round of whom little was known.

Despite no wins in any previous World Cup final matches stretching back to 1954, Scotland started as strong favourites and Willie Ormond's side went ahead through a Peter Lorimer goal on 26 minutes.

The Tartan Army section of the 25,800 crowd watching in the Westfalen Stadium were soon cheering again as Joe Jordan made it 2-0 seven minutes later. Though there was a brief flood-light failure, there was little else of note in the first half. In such a tough group, it was expected Scotland would go for broke in the second half and try and rack up as big a winning margin as possible in case goal difference ultimately decided the group. However,